CALTON HILL

Regent Gardens

Royal Observatory

National Monument
(Unfinished)

Nelsons Monument
at base 335 at summit 480

Dugald Stewarts Mont.

High School of Edinburgh

REGENT TERRACE

NORTH BRITISH RAILWAY

Tunnel Entrance

West Division

Edinburgh Prison

Middle Division

East Division

Calton Old Burial Ground

Governors House

CALTON NEW BURIAL GROUND

ABBEY STRAND

Queen Marys Bath

Burns Monument

Brewery

Craig End

Amphion Place

Tunnel Entrance

NORTH BACK OF CANONGATE

Brewery

Brewery

Brewery

Site of Pauls Work

Gasometer

ROYAL STABLES

Brewery

MACDOWALL STR.

Fish Market

Edinburgh Gas Works

Chimney
base to summit 329 ft.

Grave Yard

Hospital

House of Refuge

Hospital

GOODS STATION
(North British Railway)

Canongate Board School

Christian Instn.

Board School

Free Church Normal School

N Tolbooth

Canongate Tolbooth

Milton House School

Queensberry Lodge

Holyrood Glass Wks

High School
Cricket

JEFFREY STREET

Trinity College Church

John Knox's Free Ch.

Netherbow Port

John Knox's Ho.

St. Marys Brewery

Moray Ho.

Free Church
Normal School

Moray Free Ch.

Brewery

Brewery

Holyrood Square

SOUTH BACK OF CANONGATE

Ale Stores

Gasometer

Gasometer

HOLYROOD

DUMBIEDYKES

Mission Hall

St Patricks R.C Chapel

R.C School

St Anns R.C

St Mary's Brewery

ST JOHNS STREET

St Johns Pl.

St Johns Ch.

Reids Courts

Prince Albert Buildings

Albert Buildings

Queens Terrace

BLACKFRIARS STREET

ST. MARYS STREET

St Johns Hill

Tannery

ST JOHN'S HILL

Long Close

Brewery

Prospect Place

PROSPECT PLACE

HIGH SCHOOL YARDS

Fever Hospital

City Hospital

Bath

Public Baths

Old Town Wall

Board School

INFIRMARY STREET

DRUMMOND STREET

ROXBURGH STREET

EAST ADAM STREET

WEST ADAM STREET

NORTH RICHMOND STREET

ARTHUR STREET

Friends Meeting Ho.

Burial Ground

Royal College Surgeons

COLLEGE STREET

University of Edinburgh

Theatre

BURY CRAGS

ARTHUR STREET

Bartholomew
150 years

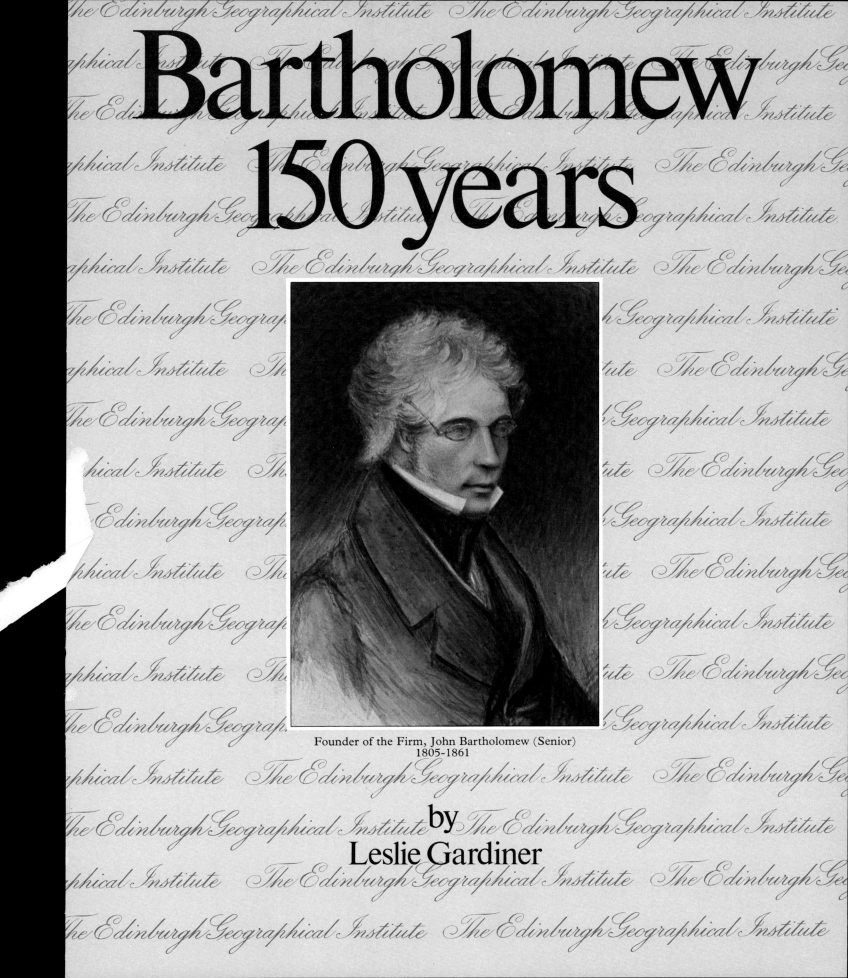

Founder of the Firm, John Bartholomew (Senior)
1805-1861

by
Leslie Gardiner

Acknowledgements

© 1976 John Bartholomew & Son Ltd
Printed and Published by
John Bartholomew & Son Ltd,
Edinburgh, Scotland.
Text written by Leslie Gardiner
Book Design by Forth Studios Ltd
of Edinburgh.
Reproduction by Friarsgate Studio Ltd
of Beverley.
Typesetting in Plantin 110
and Times New Roman
Paper – Chromomatt 135 gsm
Printed on a Roland 800 4-colour
offset Litho press
Book Bound by
Hunter & Foulis Ltd, Edinburgh
ISBN O-84152 791 A

Contents

Foreword

So often it is the intention of successive generations to record, for posterity, the history of their own times, and so often these good intentions have been thwarted by other commitments and meanwhile, 'old father time' just keeps rolling along. In the 1920's, as manuscript notes suggest, my father obviously wished to do just such a thing to mark the firm's centenary.

Now, for our 150th anniversary, this history of the firm has become a reality. This has come about by commissioning the well-known and gifted writer Leslie Gardiner who, as author of the book, has been able to devote his professional talents in bringing together a wealth of fascinating material which has been stored by many successive Bartholomews, all of whom have inherited the squirrel instinct. Mr Gardiner is to be congratulated on producing a charming and romantic story which, although in essence is a history of the firm and its cartographic development, is also a most readable chronicle of the times.

Mention should also be made of Forth Studios, who, in designing this book, have managed to make a history into an attractive and exciting visual production, aided by the efforts of Friarsgate Studio, who have been responsible for the colour reproduction.

The book itself speaks for the devotion of countless employees, who through their skilled crafts have applied their working lives in faithfully and attractively recording history on the map. This is also an appropriate place to pay tribute to the Bartholomew staff, both past and present who have continued and still maintain this tradition of excellence.

4th June 1976

Peter H Bartholomew
Chairman

List of Illustrations & Photographs

1 Old Times

Reducing part of Persia, twice...12s 6d
Finishing off North Germany..£7 5s 0d
Reducing ancient Rome..£1 10s 0d

- the scraps of paper might be the accounts rendered by some latter-day Genghis Khan, ruthless in conquest but extremely moderate in his charges. They represent, however, the first rough work sheets of John Bartholomew of Edinburgh, a jobbing engraver just out of his time and, in the opinion of those who deal with him, a 'busy little man' (height five feet six). They are dated 1826 and they are our first glimpse of what will one day be the house of Bartholomew. (John's grandson incorporated the date 1820 in the emblem of his firm, but that very likely marked the start of the founder's apprenticeship at the age of fifteen.)

John is not the first of his line in Scotland. There have been Bartholomews of Linlithgow and Kirkliston, West Lothian, and afterwards over in Fife, since at least the mid-1600s. Nor is he the first to adopt the rather recondite craft of engraver: his father has been engraving art work for Lizars' of Edinburgh since 1797, eight years before John was born. But he is the first to specialise in map engraving. Over the next thirty years he will join the pantheon of pioneers. He will found the house of Bartholomew and confirm Edinburgh as a metropolis of map-makers. A hundred and fifty years on, his firm alone will be found maintaining Edinburgh's map-making reputation.

Cartography was not long out of the here-be-dragons era when John's father joined Lizars' but it was being recognised as an occupation peculiarly suited to Scotsmen. It attracted men with an infinite capacity for taking pains, master-craftsmen with that 'energy, audacity and tact combined, of which (Arnold Bennett has written) some Scotsmen seem to possess the secret.' Names which shine from the dark origins of map-making are mostly Scottish: Timothy Pont, Robert Gordon, John Adair, John Ogilby . . . the last, born in Edinburgh, cosmographer-royal to King Charles II, pushed his measuring wheel all over England's roads and was compiling a *Geographical Description of the World* when he died.

In cartographical engraving, Edinburgh has a traceable history.* John Clarke, 'an engraver of Edinburgh', inscribed the 'Towne & Water of Montrose' on copper for John Adair's book on the Scottish coasts and islands in 1698. Twenty years later Richard Cooper founded a school of engraving in Edinburgh and one of his pupils was Andrew Bell, better known as a co-founder of the *Encyclopaedia Britannica* (for which Bartholomew's would one day do the maps and plans).

Bell's apprentice was Daniel Lizars, himself a notable engraver of the next generation – he was responsible for a historic Plan of Leith in 1806. Daniel Lizars' pupil was George

Engraver's Tools

Copper Plate Press

*Traced by Dr Ian H. Adams in his paper *The Edinburgh School of Geographical Engravers*

Bartholomew; and George's son John was indebted to that firm for a start in business on his own account – a freelance engraver, a superior tradesman who followed a craft of which the origins go back to the middle ages.

As etching developed out of the armourer's art, so engraving came from the goldsmith's. The raw material is copper but, about the time John Bartholomew sets up his work bench, steel plates are coming into fashion. They are hard, and they get rusty, but their big disadvantage, for map engravers, is that you cannot make corrections on them.

John, therefore, takes his short steel 'graver' with its pointed, wedge - or diamond-shaped head, and on a copper plate he cuts lines and furrows, broad and narrow, deep and shallow, according to the light and shade requirements of the picture or map he is engraving. It is incredible, what myriads of fine lines and shadings a gifted engraver can produce for a map, what a wealth of baroque decoration and intricate lettering he can create.

When the map has been copied and checked over, John heats his copper plate and rubs his stick of ink over it. The ink melts into the engraved furrows. The rest he wipes off. Then the plate goes into a hand press (a sophisticated novelty for its day, a clumsy archaism by twentieth-century standards) with a sheet of paper on it, and he passes it back and forth between the rollers. The versatile engraver runs off as many copies as are required and afterwards he colours each copy with his paints, or more often gets someone else to colour it. (In Edinburgh it was a popular occupation for decayed gentlewomen and spinsters with time on their hands.)

While this is going on they have opened, let us say, the London & Birmingham Railway (1838). John must grave it in for the next edition. He beats out his plate on his tiny anvil and redraws the section. Some day, but perhaps not for years, the old copper plate will be so full of amendments that he will have to scrap it and engrave a new one. That is the occupational hazard of the cartographical engraver, for a map is a living thing, not like a picture or a testimonial but a reflection of the progress of mankind, graved in and beaten out on the surface of a copper plate.

John's graving tools, anvil and parallel rulers are homemade. Some have come down to him from old-time engravers and some he will pass on to his descendants. (In 150 years' time you will be able to see them in the offices of the firm which will bear his name.) The plates he engraves will be museum-pieces if posterity manages to preserve and identify them – but it may not do so. From modesty, or lack of time, or because most of the work is sub-contracted to him, John Bartholomew leaves few signed or monogrammed plates behind him.

He signs the work sheets. On tattered fragments the entries continue:

'Engraving and Outline, Hills and Coasting of Egypt......................£4
Reducing and Engraving Colombia, on Steel............................£8
Reducing Plan of Disputed Marches for Mr Gellatly......................4s'

In his first independent year, John's total earnings are £78 16s 6d and in his second £112 14s. Most of this is paid to him by Lizars' for a variety of jobs: reducing, engraving and lettering the towns and counties of Scotland, inscribing the occasional medal and silver presentation watch, making name-plates for citizens' doors, engraving visiting cards (a growth industry in genteel quarters), decorating spoons and snuff-boxes.

One more piece of letter paper is enough for the profit and loss account of the first six years: income £643, expenditure £459.

Edinburgh is becoming a city of printers but there are not many first-class engravers about and John is recognised as one of the more diligent and reliable. The rate at which he builds a reputation in these slow-moving times is quite astonishing. Here is a letter from Gray & Son of Glasgow, dated November 1828. (John is twenty-three. Two years ago he was an apprentice boy.)

'Dear Sir,

'We write this to solicit a very particular favour and hope that you will not refuse it. You know that we had Mackie here at these maps of which you did some, and we wish to God you had Engraved the whole of them, he worked in his own room and was paid cash occasionally, having a price to put upon each according to the labour when finished – from indolence or some other cause he made but slow progress while we foolishly allowed him to draw cash – until we found he had *overdrawn* for all that he intended he should do – but the most foolish thing in us was we had permitted him to do several of them only partially . . . .

'At last finding he could get no more money he suggested that as Mr Lizars wished him to Edinr he would take them with him, finish them and forward them one or two at a time as they were done – we saw no other way to get rid of him and . . . assented to the proposal, trusting to some portion of honour or honesty – weeks and months elapsed and no plates came, while we were occasionally writing him angry letters – he on the 1st of last month pled ill health as the cause and promising to have two of them West next week – but none has yet come – we can be fooled no longer and have wrote to a Man of Business in Edinr to get them or force them out of his hands, and have now to ask if you would have the goodness to take in hand the finishing them, and we would forward to you with the originals and instructions as soon as they reach us – they are now Urgently wanted, at least some of them – we regret exceedingly that we ever employed that fellow Mackie . . . .

'We hope and trust that you will be able to accomplish this and shall cheerfully and liberally pay your charges, we expect more to follow, which you shall have . . . .

'P.S. If you would add the following to the Map herewith sent and fill up from the mouths of the Danube up the river Pruth taking in part of Galicia and Poland as marked with pencil beyond Warsaw . . . also add under vignette in small letters "Beautiful Palace of Moscow".'

John is able to help his clients out of this hole and a subsequent letter mentions that 'from the superior manner in which all your former (works) are executed, Messrs Blackie & Co. wishes us to take in hands all the remaining ones which are to do. If therefore you could find any person you could trust we would feel obliged . . . but we wish it to be understood that you should superintend the Engraver and make your own charge.'

Perhaps this letter, and one or two like it, persuade John that he might do well to take an apprentice. By the 1830s his name appears to be made in his native city at least – letters are arriving addressed simply: 'Mr John Bartholomew, Engraver, Edinburgh.'

His earliest published work, as far as we know, was a Directory Plan for Edinburgh. A landmark in Scottish cartography, it was done for W. & D. Lizars in 1826 and was the first of many city plans which the future house of Bartholomew would produce. A hundred years on it would be printed again in the Edinburgh & Leith Postal Directory, to give citizens of 1926 a useful idea of the town their forefathers lived in – woodland where the Usher Hall rises, the four fingers of the 'Earthen Mound' menacing Princes Street, the city markets spread over what was not yet Waverley station.

George Bartholomew 1784–1871

From John's work sheets of the 1830s we see that he has a hand in the range of Scottish guide-books published by Adam & Charles Black and in Lizars' big *Edinburgh Geographical General Atlas*. A quaint relic of 1839 is his engraving of one page of the late Sir Walter Scott's manuscript of *Ivanhoe*. He secures the commission for the *Encyclopaedia Britannica* map work, which his descendants will hold for the next ninety-odd years.

In the 1840s he is busy with a series of schoolroom maps for the Scottish School Book Association – a venture into a potentially profitable and exacting world, the world of educational map and atlas publishing. No one at that date can foresee the steady expansion of that business, or its culmination towards the end of the century in an immense tide of school maps and atlases; on the crests of which the house of Bartholomew will triumphantly ride.

In the years of struggle John lives and works at 4 East St James Street, at the east end of Edinburgh's Princes Street, in sordid surroundings and dignified company. The famous publishing houses of Constable and Ballantyne are nearby (the former going spectacularly broke in the year he finishes his apprenticeship). An exciting new publication, *Blackwood's Edinburgh Magazine,* is issued at the same end of Princes Street. (Some time soon, Blackwood's and Bartholomew's will co-operate to produce a handsome series of county maps, each folded inside a stiff, pocket-sized cover, which will wear and keep their neatness and freshness for a century or more.)

Round the corner in Leith Walk the brothers Chambers (W. & R.) sleep under the counter, acting as nightwatchmen of their own small shop.

The New Town fringe is a hotbed of vigorous small-time 'steam' printers and associated tradesmen. The literary, social and political life of the capital washes to its gates and, if John is not too preoccupied hachuring the Alps, he may see among his neighbours' visitors a foppish young stranger his own age (Benjamin Disraeli,

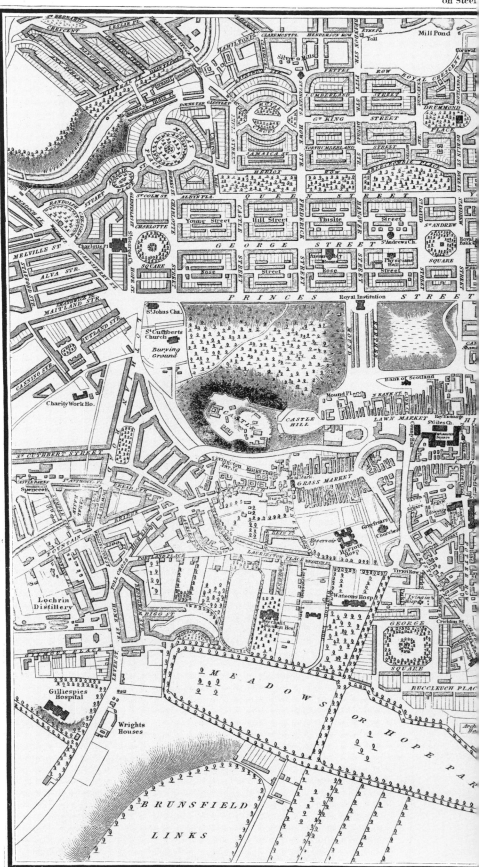

Directory Plan of Edinburgh 1826. Drawn
and engraved by John Bartholomew
(Senior) for W & H Lizars

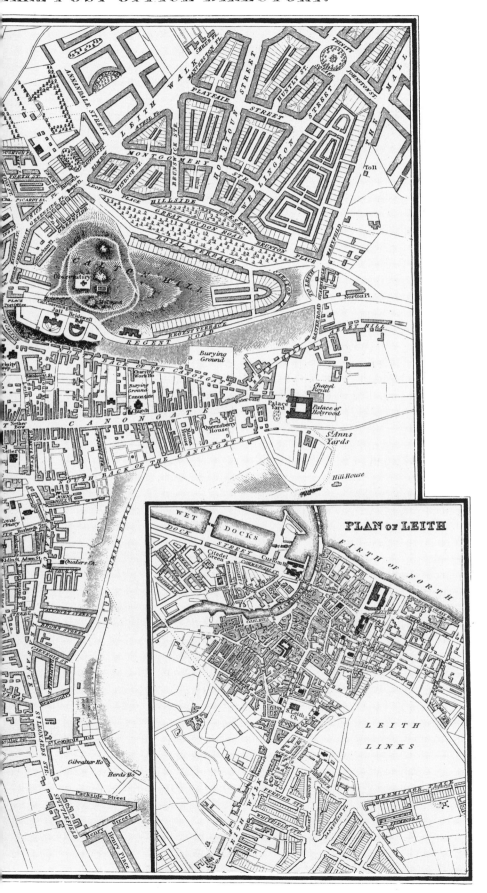

PLAN OF LEITH

looking for a new editor for the *Quarterly Review* in 1826) – a grubby old man in a stovepipe hat (J.M.W. Turner, no stranger to the copper plate and the reducing glass, discussing the engraving of his landscapes for Scott's *Collected Poems*) – a buoyant German lad and a pale, long-haired Italian (Mendelssohn in 1829 and Paganini in 1831) at the door of Paterson's the music publisher's – and the Wizard of the North himself, broken in health and

North Bridge 1859-1870 looking south from Princes Street, Bartholomew Printing Premises on left

financially ruined by the Constable collapse.

The building boom continues, the New Town of Edinburgh spreads north and many an ambitious businessman moves with it. In 1855 John Bartholomew is at 59 York Place, married with five children. There he employs his son Henry (born 1834) and five engravers and apprentices who live, in the old tradition, as members of the Bartholomew family and go for a week's holiday every year to the Bartholomew cottage at Dreghorn, under the Pentland Hills. John finds employment for independent journeymen too, one of whom is his father George – sixty years an engraver, not to figure in the history of the firm but secure in his reputation as producer of the Plan of Leith for John Wood's massive *Town Atlas of Scotland* (1818-1830) and the Edinburgh street plans of 1825 and 1829, published by J. Lothian of St Andrew Square.

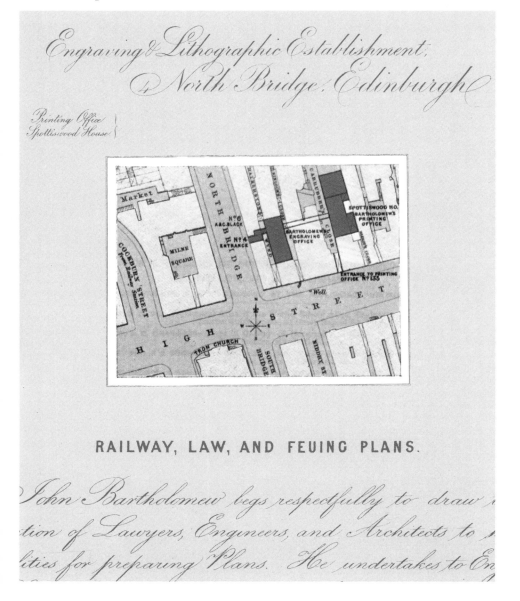

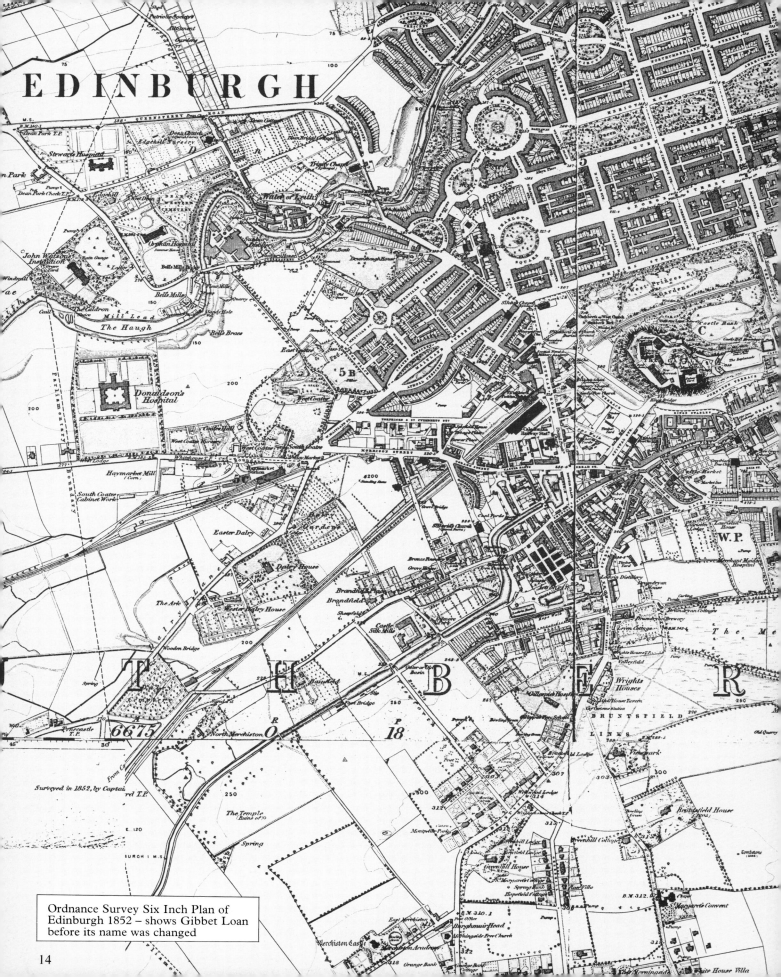

EDINBURGH

Ordnance Survey Six Inch Plan of
Edinburgh 1852 – shows Gibbet Loan
before its name was changed

14

15

John is now John senior. His eldest son bears the same name and has been brought up to be a draughtsman as well as an engraver. Twenty years in the business have taught John senior the advantages of having the drawing work done on his own premises.

John junior (born 1831) has been furthering his studies in London. His father keeps watch over him:

'Be on your guard as to strangers and I may mention that Mr.Milne who went to London on the same day as you had his pocket picked of several pounds notwithstanding he is such a precise man'

– and keeps him informed about business developments:

'There has been a great meeting of the working classes about obtaining a half holiday on Saturdays.'

The young man talks of going to Germany, but John senior advises against it and tells him there is a partnership waiting for him at home. What a grand thing it will be, writes John junior's brother, in jest but with a prophetic insight he is not aware of, when 'you set up large premises with Father and get on like Johnston* or some of these great engravers . . . .'

John Bartholomew senior lives to see his firm flourishing at its first separate commercial address, 'two large rooms and a closet for £12 per annum'** at 4 North Bridge, opposite the *Scotsman* office. He also lives to see Edinburgh increase its importance as a centre of the printing and publishing trades which are bound to influence the future of cartography and map engraving. For some time his health has been failing and in 1859 he relinquishes control of the business to John junior and retires to Grangebank Cottage in Morningside, south of the city.

On a spring day two years later he begins his last official letter in a shaky travesty of his careful hand:

'Gentlemen, I hereby acknowledge . . . .'

There the writing tails off and underneath it, in the thin crabbed script of a worn-out man, is a note to his son:

'Dear John, I find myself utterly incapable of writing or spelling at present you must do it yourself JB.'

The founder of the house of Bartholomew dies on 9th April 1861.

*W. & A. K. Johnston of Edinburgh, founded 1825, famous for maps in the last century
**John Bartholomew's letter of 11th May 1859

2 Engravings & Lithography Neatly Executed

Watching the shop-boy in North Bridge polishing up the brass plate of the Edinburgh Engraving & Lithographic Establishment, a knowledgeable man-about-Edinburgh might reflect that this was a somewhat high-faluting title for a business which, within recent memory, had been a one-man jobbing engraver's. But John Bartholomew could justify it by pointing to his wages bill which, in the year his father died (1861), was running at £1000 a year. The figure implies that he employed a staff of about twenty.

Lithography, the firm's new title indicates, had been added to engraving. Lithography was a method of reproducing drawings, paintings and printed matter from a stone instead of a metal plate, a technique barely half a century old.

Lithography works on the principle that oil and water do not mix. Artists used greasy chalks, acid and gum and much inking and washing of the lithographic stone . . . a messy operation, one supposes, yet in the hands of a master it gave, and still gives, most beautiful results.

When maps were lithographed they were first 'pulled' on transfer paper from the copper engraving. To the transfer a 'patcher' added borders, scales and notes and set the page for its application, in a delicate operation, to the stone. From the humble-sounding 'patchers' of yesterday has come the highly-skilled editorial department of today.

For coloured maps, several separate transfers had to be made, and the stone was prepared for its colours by a 'colourist'. Bartholomew's were uniquely ahead of their time in this department (which was picturesquely known as 'Tint Stones'), for they always employed girls.

After careful inspection by John Bartholomew himself, the gummed-up stone was trundled to the press and propelled back and forth under the rollers. If the first 'pulls' showed no inaccuracies, printing went ahead at full speed. One of the girls spent forty-five minutes feeding in a ream of paper – 500 sheets – and could then get on with her knitting for fifteen minutes while a printer washed and gummed-up the stone for another ream. This went on all day, the eight hours producing a steady 4000 impressions.

The girls of 'Tint Stones', females in a man's world, did not find a union to look after them until 1969, when they were accepted by the Society of Litho Artists, Designers and Engravers.

Handling the flat, polished stones was the laborious part of lithography. The biggest weighed nearly a ton apiece and all had to be moved about on trolleys and manoeuvred painfully into position in the bed of the printing machine. They were limestones, quarried only at Solenhofen in Bavaria. They lasted a lifetime: having scored a design in the surface, you could smooth it away when you no longer needed it by scrubbing it with various grades of abrasive brick. Scrubbing, scraping, checking for smoothness with ruler and tissue paper might take an experienced polisher ten or twelve hours. It was not until 1926, when the lithographic stone

was becoming obsolete, that the invention of the 'levigator' belatedly rendered polishing easy.

Chronologically, Bartholomew's were not in the front rank of lithographers.

'I don't think Father is favourable to the engaging of the stone engraver,' John junior's brother informed him in May 1854. 'He says he could not get work to keep him going, as there is nothing but off-hand things done on stone . . . . So, John, you see you will have to "urge your claim" a little farther before you will get Father to agree with you. I was asking him, if he he thought stone engraving so much inferior to the copper, how Mr P. got so much work at it. I think if you were writing Father shewing him that you could get work he would not be against engaging the German.

'Don't let on though that I have sent you this . . . .'

The North Bridge office, the firm's first business address, shared a building with A. & C. Black the publishers, who had helped set John senior on his feet. Down the years the two firms have run in parallel: the respective heads of the two firms then were the great-grandfathers of the respective chairmen of the two firms today.

Black's are renowned nowadays as the publishers of *Who's Who*. By a coincidence, Bartholomew's other close connection of the 1850s was with the publishers of the *Who's Who* of European royalty, the *Almanac de Gotha*. This was the firm of Justus Perthes.

The house of Justus Perthes had risen in the old-fashioned ducal capital of Gotha, a typical *opéra-buffe* citadel of the Prussian states where the brass band plays every morning in the *platz*. The marriage of its ruling prince, Albert, to Queen Victoria made Gotha an appendage of the British crown. It was also a small centre of fine printing, a satellite of the Leipzig tradition.

Justus Perthes specialised in cartography and the firm's bright star was the Mr P. of the above letter: Augustus Petermann. He had met John junior on his 1848 visit to Edinburgh to do business with the rival map firm of W. & A. K. Johnston, when he was twenty-four and John seventeen.

Petermann was greatly impressed with the boy. He wanted to take him into Perthes' London office – the family thought John too young – Petermann waited seven years and asked again – this time John was granted leave to go. He spent two years there, broadening his experience and his outlook and meeting cartographers. His friendship with Herr Petermann lasted all his life and might have brought down the Bartholomew business in the second generation, for young John was tempted to emigrate to Gotha. But his father was ailing, and needed his son's shoulders to lay the burden of affairs on, and John junior relinquished that dream.

Father all his life had been an artisan, spending every day in office and workshop, taking a hand in every stage of the practical work. He proceeded cautiously, step by step. The son was more adventurous. He had had better opportunities for educating himself and mixing with the world. He saw the romance and potential of map-making and was ready to invest his future in it. Within two years of becoming head of the firm he was taking more space in the building, throwing out a wing and a bridge at the back, into Carrubber's Close, and installing two more steam presses – making a total of three. From the original drawing of a map to the printing-off of copies he could handle every cartographical process from his own resources.

John Bartholomew (Junior)

He travelled, creating new business. 'With regard to Mr John Bartholomew's abilities as a geographer & of his mechanical skill in preparing maps, I have the greatest pleasure in adding my testimony,' wrote Robert Chambers of the Edinburgh publishing house in a letter of introduction of 1863. 'The work prepared by that gentleman for this firm has given to each individual member unqualified satisfaction . . . . In every transaction Mr Bartholomew & I have acted most harmoniously, indeed he has united to the character of a geographical scholar that of a thorough gentleman & has thus won my unqualified regard.'

John's neighbour and client, Adam Black, affirmed:

'We can recommend Mr Bartholomew as an excellent practical engraver and compiler of Maps &c, thoroughly acquainted with the Minutiae of his business. He possesses an extensive and recent knowledge of geography & is most attentive to any work which he undertakes, while his charges have always appeared to us very moderate . . . .'

As to John's own letters, we detect a new note of confidence and authority. Here is a confirmation of agreement of 1865, when he took on Fullarton's *Atlas*, a cartographical milestone of that decade:

'Gentlemen,
'I hereby agree to prepare a series of 26 maps, size of the one drawn, measuring over the border line 16¼″ x 11½″ and to print the same in four colours viz. – 1 black and three coloured tints so as to give a distinctive colour to each division of a county, for the sum of 2d per map or 4d per part of two maps. The paper to be furnished by you.
'I also agree to prepare written copy for separate indexes to each map and also for general index to the whole book without extra charge, but on the condition that I have a right to obtain a cast from your plates of general index. It is to be understood that you are to sell the work in parts and only by canvassing and not to the regular bookselling trade. You are to have the sole right to publish the separate descriptive index to each map during the seven years of your guarantee, and the publishers of the entire book, Messrs A. & C. Black, are only to have a right to the general index . . . .
'The terms of payment to be the same as in the 7th article of Agreement for Imperial Map of England & Wales. The written copy of indexes to be furnished by me in same condition as for the *Royal Illustrated Atlas* and arranged alphabetically by you . . . .'

Fullarton's went bankrupt, and such failures were not

Illustrations for a botanical text-book produced in 1881

Red or Corn Poppy

uncommon, but those were golden days of opportunity for men of energy and credit in the printing world. It is hard to think of any major social, political or economic development of the latter half of the nineteenth century which did not put orders in their books. Lithography, for example, a process which few knew the meaning of when John junior adopted it, turned out to be essential for the printing of cheque-books when the banks introduced them and for the reproduction of diagrams for the medical, biological and botanical text-books which the advance of scientific education called into being. Railway mania had run its course, but still the railways proliferated and every new line required plans and illustrated prospectuses and none were better equipped for drawing them up and reproducing them in quantity than cartographers and geographical engravers. Each new rail network rendered a few county maps and town plans obsolete and booksellers up and down the country reported that customers for maps asked one question only: "Has it got the level crossings on it?"

Old Bartholomew hands must have recalled with a smile the red-letter day of years gone by, when an order for five schoolroom maps came in from William Knox of the Scottish School Book Association. Education for all was now the cry. The demand for maps and atlases exceeded the most extravagant forecasts, building up to more than a million times five.

Scottish firms profited – A. & C. Black, W. & R. Chambers, Collins, Meiklejohn, Macmillan, W. & A. K. Johnston and Nelson among them – but in the minds of schoolmasters and scholars the name of Bartholomew came to be associated as closely as any with the study of geography. (Bartholomew's, however, never went in for wall-maps or globes on a large scale.)

The growth of Empire; the discovery of new territories from the heart of Africa to the Polar ice-caps; the supersession of sail by steam (it meant a revision of shipping routes); an unbroken series of wars in both hemispheres (new frontiers); electoral reform (constant re-definition of the parliamentary boundaries); the evangelical campaigns of churches and missionary societies (we do not always realise how enterprising and widespread *they* were); the invention of the penny-farthing bicycle (demanding a new type of road-map and foreshadowing the tremendous appetites of the cycling clubs for road-maps two or three decades later) . . . these are a few of the events and movements of John junior's time which showed that geography, like history, never stood still; a time of challenge which was the salvation or the ruin of map-makers, depending on how they met the challenge.

John junior's programme was chiefly cartographical. But he had a hand in some interesting one-off jobs. Anyone in Scotland with an out-of-the-way piece of mapping or engraving to do thought instantly of John Bartholomew. He displayed a flexibility of outlook which characterises the firm to the present day.

Under Robert Louis Stevenson's instructions, he drew the

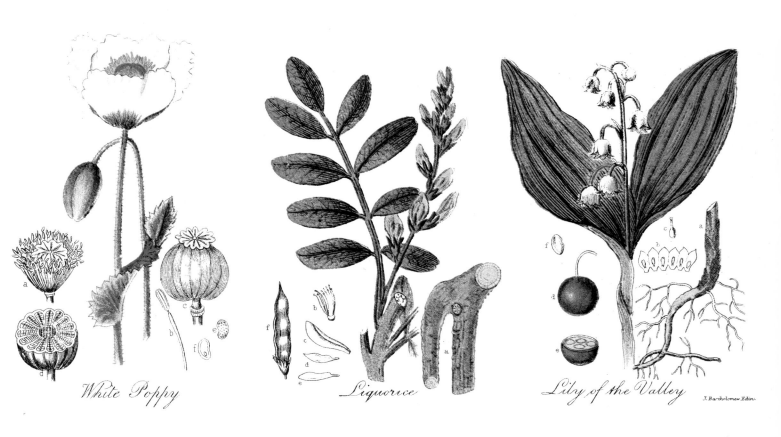

White Poppy.

Liquorice.

Lily of the Valley.

J. Bartholomew Edin.

Calamint.

J. Bartholomew Edin.

Peony.

Pennyroyal.

J. Bartholomew Edin.

BLACKWOOD'S
COUNTY MAPS
—
SUTHERLAND

J.B., Aug. 1846

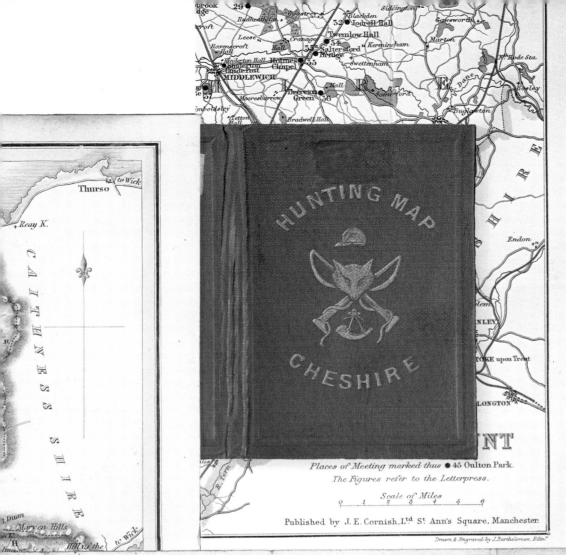

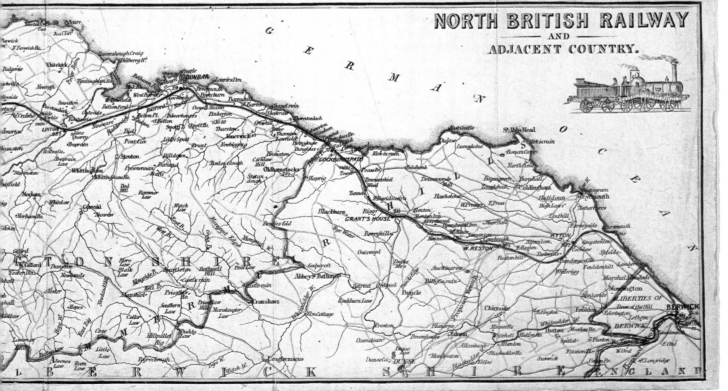

ever-memorable map of Treasure Island for a frontispiece to the first edition of the book. How many times it has been reproduced is a figure no bibliophile could state to the nearest ten thousand. *Treasure Island* would not be *Treasure Island* without that evocative island plan and its 'Spye Glafs Hill' and 'Cape of ye Woods', delineated by 'Billy Bones', with latitude and longitude 'struck out by J. Hawkins'. Running a hand over the worn old copper plate in the Bartholomew archives, one hears an echo from childhood of the tap of Blind Pew's stick and the parrot's cry: "Pieces of Eight! Pieces of Eight!"

John drew on stone the official 'artist's impression' of the Forth Railway Bridge, designed as the most imposing civil engineering work of the century. A copy of the engraving hangs in a room at the firm's Edinburgh headquarters today, aesthetically interesting, historically a rarity, for it depicts the bridge that never was – the bridge which was scrapped, and its designer dismissed.

In the 1870s there were dozens of map-making and map-publishing firms, some short-lived; and, although Scotland had more than her share, Edinburgh was not the only metropolis of maps. Large firms had their London offices. George Philip's, one of the more soundly-based, was in Liverpool. Its head, George Philip himself, was John Bartholomew's sister-in-law's brother-in-

law and in 1879 he put out feelers about a merger. John reacted coolly – he preferred Edinburgh to Liverpool, he said. Mr Philip replied with an offer of partnership in a new joint business in London. But John's reluctance stemmed from other considerations than a comparison of cities (he perhaps feared being swallowed up) and he rejected the idea.

> 'Of course I accept your decision as final,' George Philip wrote, 'and you must excuse my having been somewhat persistent in pressing the matter upon you, which I did from no motive of personal advantage, but for a desire to make our interests identical . . . .'

John's most vivid innovation in the science of map-making was his introduction in the first commercial series of maps of what was called 'contour layer colouring'. The maps of his father's day had been given artistically-coloured outlines and coloured boundary lines, but the body of a map was traditionally blank except for the black lettering which filled it up. Hachuring – an engraving modification of relief shading – had replaced the antiquated convention of relief signs – where a mountain, for instance, had been represented by a drawing of a small mound. But even with hachuring it was not possible to give proper ideas of steepness and height, however diligent and ingenious the engraver. The map of the Scottish Highlands, cluttered with peaks and undulations, looked when hachured as though a colony of moles had been busy under it. The long Apennine chain resembled a centipede; but how tall, and how steep-sided, could not be made clear.

Then came contours to replace the hachures: thin wavering lines all over the map, marking the intervals of 100, 200 or perhaps 500 feet, supplying a truer picture of the configuration of a landscape. And then, towards the end of the 1870s, came John Bartholomew's contour layer colouring, each step of 100 feet or so (the intervals varied in the series he first made famous with it) having its own colour. There were delicate tints of green and brown for the plains and foothills, shading to deep brown and purple for the highlands and touches of white for the Matterhorns and Jungfraus. He extended the system to cover the seas: pale blue denoted shallow water, the darkest ultramarine the profound depths of ocean trenches.

To the casual student of a map, very pretty; but not the most startling of inventions? You had to be a cartographer, a printer or an engraver to appreciate what it meant technically. Colours, in John junior's day, had to be applied one at a time in separate printings. With the equipment then available it required no ordinary skill to keep a colour within the precise limits, which might be the merest fraction of an inch apart.

Contour layer colouring, therefore, gave one a good idea of a terrain at a glance, and emphasised new standards of accuracy. John put the maps on show at the Paris Exhibition of 1878, where they attracted some attention, most of it unfavourable. Cartographers of the period, notoriously conservative, seemed to

Top left: Frontispiece illustration for R L Stevenson's Treasure Island, 1st edition 1883, engraved for Cassells

Bottom left: 'The Bridge that never was' a lithograph in eight colours of the original design for the Forth Railway Bridge abandoned in 1879 following the Tay Bridge disaster. Designed by Sir Thomas Bouch MICE, Engineer
Total length of Bridge 1½ miles
Length of two Great Spans 1600 feet each, or about ⅓ of a mile
Height of Bridge above High Water 150 feet
Height of the Towers above High Water 600 feet
Total weight of Chains 6000 tons

Black's ¼ inch map of Scotland 1862

consider it a catchpenny trick, liable to take the mystique out of geography and make it intelligible to laymen.

By this time the Bartholomew plant was in new premises. 'The diminutive and obscure *place* called Brown's Square,' says Scott★, 'was hailed about the time of its erection as an extremely elegant improvement upon the style of designing and erecting Edinburgh residences. Each house was, in the phrase used by appraisers, "finished within itself" or, in the still newer phraseology, "self-contained". It was built about the year 1763-4 . . . .'

Number 17 was the firm's new address. John put his steam engines in an annexe built out over the yard; the once-fashionable reception rooms of eighteenth-century Edinburgh became the workshops; and John's private office was the salon depicted in the well-known painting (but incorrectly) as the meeting-place of Burns and Scott.

During the Bartholomew occupancy, the Post Office changed the address to 31 Chambers Street. The Dental School and Hospital now stands on that site.

In his Chambers Street period, John owned three flat-bed steam-driven printing presses capable of handling three paper sizes. Besides engravers, draughtsmen, lithographers and printers he employed colourists, polishers and patchers . . . a staff of thirty-eight who required a total outlay of £33 in wages for a fifty-hour week. He paid his foreman £3 a week and his journeymen between £1 and £2.★★

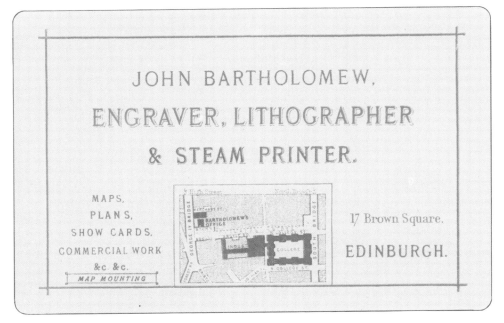

Into Chambers Street, among the printing machinery and paper stocks, the copper plates and lithographic stones, the ruling

★*Redgauntlet*, Letter II
★★Wage-bill of 1898: £91 (102 employees). Wage-bill of 1976: £10,000 (200 employees), for a forty-hour week

Opposite: 17 Brown Square 1870-1889

machines and tracing sheets and pens, drawing inks and paints and the multifarious implements of the draughtsmen and the engravers, came a new Bartholomew: John George, eldest child of John junior, fourth of the engraving Bartholomews and third of the map-making line. He was born in 1860.

Nine years after his debut in the firm he would be its head, and in the meantime he often found himself in sole charge, as his father's perambulations among foreign clients grew wider and more frequent. In 1885, armed with credentials from the American consul at Leith and the secretary of the Merchant Company of Edinburgh, John toured the United States and cemented a solid link between Bartholomew's and the New World.

In 1887, Queen Victoria's jubilee year, it was John George's turn to show the flag abroad while on a Scandinavian holiday. A paternal letter is worth quoting for its historical vignette and its evidence of that close personal and business tie between older and younger generations with which the Bartholomews were always blessed:

'My dear John George,
'I got your letter from Aberdeen and now I suppose it is time to write to Bergen. You are fortunate in getting such glorious weather as it is simply perfect though many are objecting to the hot sun . . . . Our Jubilee night passed off very well and the bonfires were seen all round to great advantage. Over *40* were seen from the Calton Hill – Arthur's Seat was a fine blaze . . . the children enjoyed the sight till after 11 and were greatly pleased. I sent the Maps to Keltie and had a note from him this morning asking if the whole of the Red. Ord. [Reduced Ordnance] Scotland were published as he had not seen more than half a dozen sheets, and also asking if the Pocket Atlases of England and Scotland were not yet ready. I have written to him today and also sent him an *entire* set of the Red. Ord. (30 sheets) and a copy of each of the Pocket Atlases England & Scotland. I had a visit from a Dr Haviland yesterday about disease maps . . . .'

The reference to disease maps suggests that John was toying with an idea – revolutionary then, taken for granted now – that to the familiar physical and political features of the contents of atlases there might be added 'special maps' to show, for example, the influence of climate on population and health. It was the germ of an idea that his son would most assiduously cultivate.

Retiring in 1888, John Bartholomew junior looked back on forty years of a career which had seen notable changes in society and science and the practice of cartography. For masses of people, reading a map was no longer as formidable an ordeal as conversing in a strange language. Geography had ceased to be the study of an exclusive academic élite. It was in the curricula of schools and young working men might be seen in public libraries, turning the pages of an atlas as though it were an exciting picture-book. (In high places, there was still room for improvement. Around that period, the War Office ordered a troopship to 'anchor off Pretoria'; a Balkan sovereign wished the French envoys 'a fair wind to Vienna'; and the Board of Admiralty, unable to decide what the capital of Madagascar was called, sent for the Hydrographer of the Navy, who not only did not know but had to confess that none of his staff knew either.)

On the practical level, John Bartholomew had enriched his firm's traditions and confirmed its reputation for accurate, painstaking cartography and had raised the status of his profession.

Thanks to him, everyone who has done a little geography at school knows Mount Everest for a patch of white in a massif of purple and grey, and sees the Mindanao Deep as a streak of blue-black.

He had arranged and prepared atlases which were to retain their freshness and usefulness and to mediate between conflicting cartographical fashions well into the twentieth century. He had been one of the first geographers to try to educate, as well as satisfy, the public. His *chef d'oeuvre* was probably the Reduced Ordnance series mentioned in the above letter: England and Scotland on the scales of four and two miles to the inch. That work cost him laborious years and, when finished, was years ahead of its time – a financial loss which the firm would bear for another generation, but in the end a wonderful contribution to the popularisation of maps and the pleasures and profits of studying them.

John junior's friends described him as a shy but shrewd man, unfailingly courteous and good-natured. He married twice and had eleven children. His health, like that of his father, had failed him in early middle age, though his intellect remained sharp and powerful. He died in 1893 in London, where he had gone to consult a new doctor.

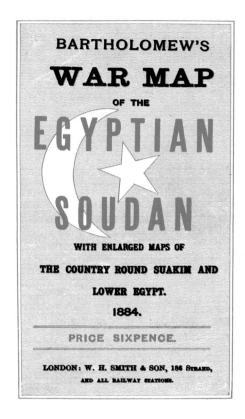

BARTHOLOMEW'S
WAR MAP
OF THE
EGYPTIAN
SOUDAN
WITH ENLARGED MAPS OF
THE COUNTRY ROUND SUAKIM AND
LOWER EGYPT.
1884.
PRICE SIXPENCE.
LONDON: W. H. SMITH & SON, 186 Strand,
AND ALL RAILWAY STATIONS.

ATLASES, MAPS, PLANS, CHARTS
and other
Geographical Illustrations
carefully Drawn & Engraved and
PRINTED PLAIN OR IN COLOUR.
RAILWAY, LAW & FEUING PLANS
Engraved or Lithographed.
Plans of Estates prepared from the Ordnance Survey.
COMMERCIAL AND BANK WORK
of every description.

3 Prince of Cartographers

"There's a man you should know who's got his head screwed on the right way in the matter of maps."

The speaker was Archibald Geikie of Edinburgh University and the listener Doctor George Chisholm, a geographer, and they were talking of John George Bartholomew, new head of the map-making firm.

Around John George (born 1860) a little cartographical

John George Bartholomew 1860-1920.
Portrait by E A Walton RSA
(On exhibition at National Portrait
Gallery, Queen Street, Edinburgh)

folklore has grown up. A former pupil of the Royal High School of Edinburgh recalls him spilling some ink, and escaping a beating for it by converting the blot into a neat map. He was famous for his sensitivity to colour harmony; an ugly or impure mixture made him feel sick. When the penny post was discontinued and the brown three-halfpenny stamp introduced, John George would have none of it but went on using the penny red with a halfpenny green, two colours he approved of.

Friends of later years hardly recognised in him the exuberant boy with a passion for outdoor activities, especially sailing and building small boats. His adult life was one long struggle against tuberculosis. Chisholm, who came to know him well, never ceased to marvel at his 'extraordinary difficulties . . . (and) extraordinary resolution . . . in constant weak, and too frequently ill, health. Sometimes he was absolutely laid aside but, except on those occasions, he went on steadily and calmly with his work.'

John George was not a man to court popularity. Affection for a few chosen friends was hidden under a grave and dignified melancholy. His close acquaintances included Sir Patrick Geddes, the Geikie brothers, Sir George Adam Smith – university and scientific colleagues before they became friends. The oceanographer Sir John Murray was another. He had been in H.M.S. *Challenger* in 1874 when she made her 'half-furtive dash'* across the Antarctic, which earned for her complement something of the prestige among scientists that veterans who had sailed with Nelson enjoyed among sailors.

When John George died, men spoke of his foresight and boldness. The boldness was early evident. On taking over from his father in 1888, he accomplished a merger with Thomas Nelson the printer and publisher and moved his firm to the low-built, spacious quadrilateral of work rooms and mock-baronial office-block called Parkside Works on a road which once bore the homely name of Gibbet Loan, on the edge of Holyrood Park. He installed four new printing machines (the largest, known as 'Jumbo', printed a four foot by five sheet) and in 1897 he put in one of the first commercial telephones: Edinburgh 611.

When he joined his father in the business, contour layer colouring was all the rage. He must have read the letters which his sisters Margaret and Matilda wrote after they had crowned their European tour of 1878 with a visit to the Paris Exhibition:

'It is a most wonderful and beautiful sight . . . we went of course to see your maps. I have as you know no individual but a great deal of *family* pride and was therefore greatly pleased and proud to find your beautifully executed maps so well represented. I think you did well in having the maps in guilded (sic) frames as that style of mounting is more in accordance with the French taste than the maple wood style as Johnston [W. & A. K.] has it . . . .'

Margaret had her own theory about the relatively cold

Life of Shackleton by Hugh Robert Mill (Heinemann, 1923)

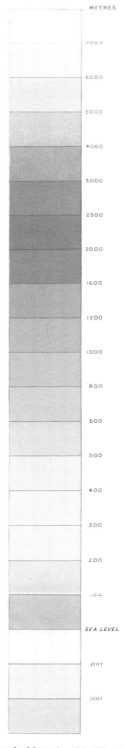

"International Map of the World" Legend
(see page 33)

ALTITUDE TINTS

METRES

7000

6000

5000

4000

3000

2500

2000

1600

1200

1000

800

600

500

400

300

200

100

SEA LEVEL

100

200

Drawn in the Geographical Section, General Staff, War Office, London, to illustrate the Conventional Signs and Styles of Type approved by the International Map Committee assembled at the Foreign Office, London, in November, 1909.
Engraved for the G.S.G.S. by Messrs John Bartholomew & Co. Edinburgh, March, 1910.

reception of layer colouring:

'We certainly think (it) merited more than "honourable mention". But at present in Paris under the Republican Government politics seem fearfully high and the fact of your having received an autograph letter from the late Emperor in praise of your maps and yourself as a celebrated geographer was quite sufficient to stamp you in politics on the side of the Emperor's party . . . . It is a wonder that your maps received any remark at all, and so absolutely must have been very good . . . .'

John George saw the first coloured maps through the press and on to the bookstalls in the pages of Baddeley's *Lake District Guide* of 1880 – a book which collectors seek for that reason. Colours were first used as a luxurious refinement in individual maps in the Half-inch series (Scotland, England and Wales) in the same decade. They were an instant success with the general public.

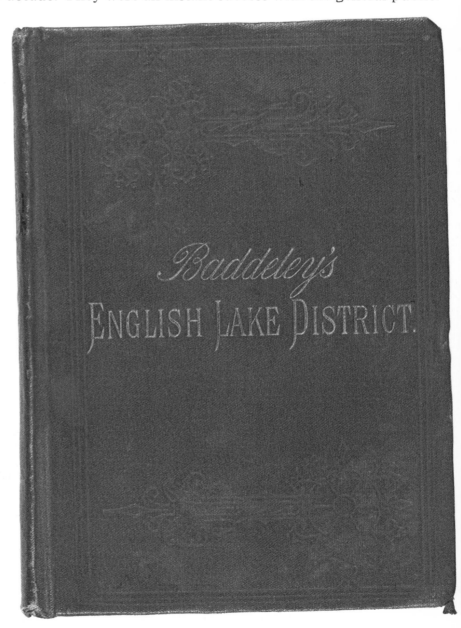

Baddeley's English Lake District. First Edition April 1880. Using 1 inch to the mile layer colouring to depict physical relief for the first time

Twenty years later, scarcely a cartographer in the world could afford to neglect layer colouring – although, as George Chisholm pointed out, 'none used it with more taste and effectiveness than the firm which invented it.' *The Times*, a quarter of a century on (22nd November 1909), would refer back to the archetypal Half-inch series when it reported on an international conference to draw up a definitive Map of the World:

'The International Map will be what is known as a hypsometric map, of which Bartholomew's tourist maps of Scotland furnish a good example. The contour lines will be drawn in brown at intervals of 100 metres .... The spaces between the contours will be tinted in green for the lower altitudes, and then in different shades of brown, increasing in darkness up to a certain altitude, where the brown merges with other tints, altitudes above 7000 metres being left white .... The sea will be shown by a blue tint, increasing in darkness according to depth ....'

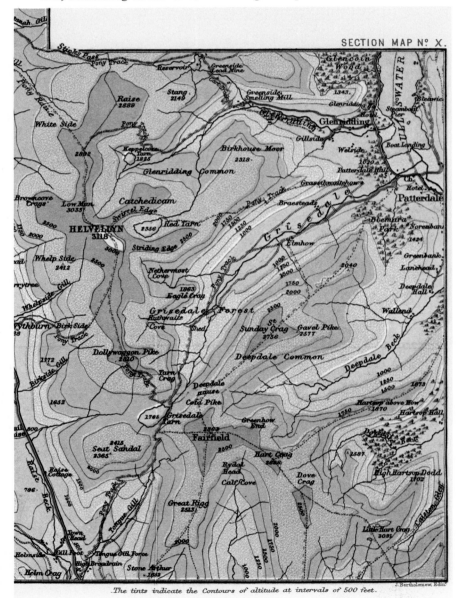

The tints indicate the Contours of altitude at intervals of 500 feet.

The year of John George's accession and amalgamation with Nelson (1888) make a watershed in the firm's history. Old times lie on one side – archaic conventions, modest operations in back rooms, dependence on neighbouring printers and publishers for a livelihood. On the other side, the Edinburgh Geographical Institute (the name fixed on his business by John George) trends away towards modern times, and the sun shines brightly on it.

Three small printing machines, steam-driven, had served the firm in 1888. Over the next twenty years, John George increased that number to fourteen, all flat-beds, the new ones gas-powered.

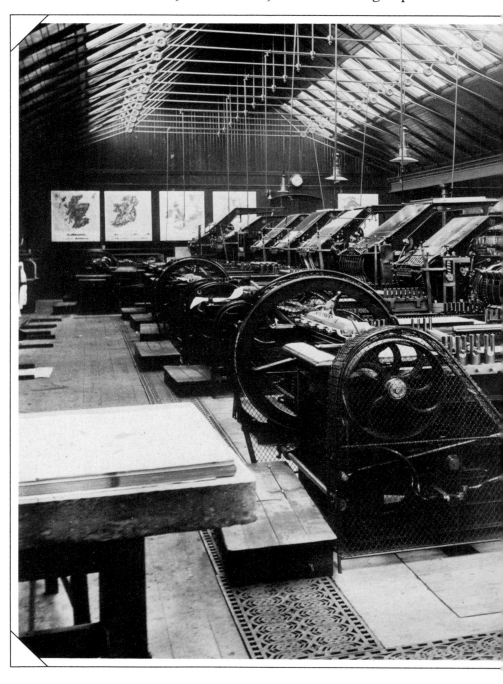

Flat bed machines at Park Road about 1890

Their value was assessed at £3,459.

The stock value of the business in 1888 included copper plates (some exist and are still in use in 1976) to the amount of £13,000. That weight of metal told a tale of variegated topography, much of it covering Scottish cities and counties in greater or lesser detail, with England and Wales almost equally well represented. The continents of Europe and America were there, complete, all their countries available separately or grouped together; and a fairly comprehensive spread of the rest of the known world – a record, scratched on metal tablets, of the geographical changes of sixty

years – a map engraver's routine collection, with here and there an exotic item (Chinese Empire, Environs of Philadelphia, Killarney Lakes) to catch the eye.

From that year on, the size and scope of operations are dramatically enlarged. The alphabetical index of customers, starting with the Automobile Club of Ceylon and ending with Yale University, grows into a calendar of commerce and administration over the world. When the new century is a few years old it includes (taking a few pages at random) the Canadian Pacific Railway, the Dundee Harbour Trust, Hachette & Cie, Russian Oil Products, the Edinburgh St Cuthbert's Co-operative Society, the India Office, British Thomson Houston, the Union Castle Line, the United Free Church of Scotland, Luxury Land Cruises Limited, the National Bible Society, the Salvation Army and Weston-super-Mare town council.

Enormous printing runs are indicated. Newnes order half a million plans of London for the next jubilee (1897) – and repeat the order. The London & North-Western Railway require 225,000 timetable maps – that is only the start of several requests for timetable maps, and the L. & N.W.R. is only one of numerous companies asking for them. Sixty thousand cycling maps, 20,000 missionary atlases, 750 sets of fifty-two maps for the *Challenger* Commission, 6,000 blotting books and maps for the Distillers Company . . . and so on, culminating in a series of orders which opens a new chapter in Bartholomew history: 260,000 patrol maps and 40,000 *Road Book of England* maps for the Automobile Association.

John George cultivated the imagination of his employees and gave it plenty to work on. It was refreshing for all to be engaged, in the space of a few months, on anatomical drawings for university text-books, wild flowers for a naturalist's *Flora*, estate plans for Scottish landowners, drainage plans for Scottish farmers, flags, maps and diagrams for encyclopaedias, the cross-sections of silver-lead mines in Sardinia, the plan and section of alterations of level for Sir Thomas Bouch's Forth Railway Bridge, tickets for a series of election addresses during Mr Gladstone's Midlothian campaign, circular maps to fit pieces of pottery made by Macintyre of Burslem . . . all in addition to the bread-and-butter map-and-atlas jobs for a galaxy of British and American publishers. The partnership with Thomas Nelson had introduced Bartholomew's to a new line of customer, while raising business with the publishing side of Thomas Nelson & Sons from £610 to £4742 in two years.

By 1891 John George had a steady relationship with some of the most respected publishers of the day – Blackwood, Dent, Methuen, John Murray. And he was doing big business with some of the giants – John Walker, Newnes, Macmillan, Cassell, Iliffe, Hodder & Stoughton, the Oxford University Press and Ward Lock.

The long-running success serial of a family firm like Bartholomew's follows a pattern. First to appear is the founder, of simple origins: diligence and honesty his stock-in-trade.

This Leaflet represents Size of Maps when folded.

The most Handy, Complete, and Reliable Series of Pocket Maps, carefully drawn from the Ordnance Survey, and corrected to date.

THE TIMES says, "Nothing better in the way of Maps."

THE

Pocket Series of Touring Maps

By J. Bartholomew. F.R.G.S.

PRICE ONE SHILLING EACH.
Mounted on Cloth and folded in Case.

LONDON:
JOHN WALKER & CO.,
Farringdon House, Warwick Lane, E.C.,
AND ALL BOOKSELLERS.

Descendants follow in orderly procession, building and consolidating. One, generally about the third generation, stands apart. It is he who, when the firm is still seeking its role in society, points it in a certain direction, shapes its future and gives it a philosophy. John George did that for Bartholomew's. Like many a semi-invalid, physically dependent on others, he displayed that individualistic courageous energy which, whether it is devoted to good or evil, mankind cannot but admire.

He took the initiative in all his affairs. Considering Gibbet Loan an inappropriate address for the Edinburgh Geographical Institute, he changed the name to Park Road on the next Edinburgh town plan – and Park Road it has remained ever since.

Off Rossdhu Point, on Loch Lomond, there are two islets,

Romantic souvenir of a boating trip when some islands were given a name one called St Winifred's and one St Rosalind's. John George Bartholomew gave them those names. While on a boating trip in that part of the loch, on a glorious June day, he came to an understanding with the girl he loved and later married – and he went home, as his diary records, in a turmoil of happy emotion over the events of 'St Winifred's Day', and on the next edition of the Half-inch Scotland (No. 7, Firth of Clyde) he commemorated St Winifred and St Rosalind for all time.

The significance of the names, however, remains a mystery. There is no Rosalind in the calendar of saints. St Winifred's Day is 3rd November, not 10th June. And his wife's name was Janet (daughter of a MacDonald of Cyder Hall, Dornoch). It must have been some private allusion that only John George, Janet and their chaperone could explain – and as far as we know they never did.

Doctor Chisholm first saw John George in a typical attitude: bent over the drawing-board at the Edinburgh Geographical Institute, parallel rulers and compasses in hand. This was one cartographer who never lost touch with the practical realities of the work, for whom the romance of map-making, like the drama of the discoveries he encouraged and recorded, never faded. Had he been fit, and not gone into maps, he might have been an explorer. The meticulous log of a windjammer's passage across the Southern Ocean, when he made a voyage to Australia for his health at the age of twenty-one, would have commended him to the leader of any expedition.

He knew several such leaders. He loved the company of explorers and all who pushed out the frontiers of knowledge. When the Commission appointed to study the findings of the *Challenger* scientists came to sit in Edinburgh (and sat so long that critics feared it had taken root), he met Lieutenant Ernest Shackleton, R.N. The same year (1884) the Royal Scottish Geographical Society held its first meeting, with John George – founder member and 'chief architect of its prosperity', as Sir Ludovic Grant described him – acting as honorary secretary.

Some years later the time came to appoint a salaried secretary. John George proposed Sir Ernest Shackleton, who wanted to get married and had to find a job.

But, says Shackleton's biographer,[*] in spite of the 'quick and open mind of Doctor John George Bartholomew the great cartographer . . . a calmness of maturity barred the Society against innovation' – in other words, it frowned on young blood. Members assembled for monthly meetings with old-world formality, wearing beards and black coats. Shackleton as secretary lounged in late, in shabby tweeds, and cracked jokes with the assistants and scattered some cigarette ash before settling down to work. Arriving early one day for a change, with his golf clubs, he started practising swings and lofted a ball through a window of the National Portrait Gallery. Shortly afterwards the hero of the Polar seas resigned.

* op. cit

It reveals something of character and temperament in John George that, while keeping the respect of stern and pompous academics, he could earn the admiration of men of action like Shackleton, Cecil Rhodes (whom he had met in Africa) and Bruce the son-in-law of David Livingstone. Two historic busts look out over the board room of the Edinburgh Geographical Institute today. One is of Augustus Petermann, friend and colleague of John George's father. The other is of H. M. Stanley, friend and colleague of John George himself.

Through such contacts he laid the foundations of the Bartholomew cartographical intelligence network and set up a correspondence with travellers, traders, missionaries and soldiers who spent their lives in remote corners of the globe. They reported to him on local topographical changes – the extension of a narrow-gauge mineral railway, the drying-up of a lake, the disappearance of a village – which might have escaped the notice of the official agencies. When he came on the scene, large areas of the world remained to be surveyed and mapped. No man knew the source of the Nile or the Amazon; the high Himalaya was unclimbed; armies in the Sudan, in the Balkans, on the North-West frontier, even in Canada and the United States, were making up their own maps as they went along (Bartholomew's pioneered military map-making during the Boer War); and the north and south Polar regions were as unexplored as the dark side of the moon.

Gordon Hayes★ credited John George with the invention of the word 'Antarctica', or at least with its resuscitation from Greek mythology: $\overset{"}{\alpha}\nu\tau\iota$ and $\overset{"}{\alpha}\rho\kappa\tau\sigma\varsigma$, meaning 'against the Bear'.

To baffle the layman of those days, one went naturally to the Greek lexicon. John George coined for himself the word 'geosopher' to express his belief that there was more to making maps than drawing them. His productions had not only to include the ordinary features of maps – relief, divisions, communications. They must also interpret conditions, show trends, disclose the interaction of climatic, social and industrial phenomena. The disease maps of Dr Haviland, which he had studied with his father, had been a tentative experiment in making maps an aid to the understanding of the earth as the cradle, the playground, the workshop and the graveyard of mankind.

By the time King Edward VII came to the throne, a Bartholomew atlas would show the world distribution of malarial regions, the incidence of child mortality, a pictorial survey of flora and fauna throughout the year, statistical comparisons of many kinds . . . down to the specialised interests of the few, such as the migratory patterns of Canadian salmon.

Early specialist maps are far from perfect and, like statistics themselves, can be misleading. John George's careful and enlightened approach helped to refine them. Take demographic

★ *Antarctica* (The Richards Press, London, 1928)

maps: the population distribution of the British Isles, say. Different colours represent so many thousands of inhabitants per square mile and the colours are arranged by counties. Staffordshire is deep red, densely populated – yet we know there are miles of rolling moorland and rural solitudes in that county. Shropshire, next door, is pale pink, no population to speak of – yet Shropshire has its industrial landscapes.

The cartographer wants to set this to rights. He takes out the large cities which distort the picture around them, and gives them a special symbol . . . then the smaller cities . . . soon his map is cluttered with symbols which require paragraphs of explanation and that is no good to those who have not time or patience to study them. He must aim at a map which gives a reasonably fair picture at a glance, plus information in depth for those who need it. Modern cartographers use considerable ingenuity in solving such problems, and they work within guide-lines which John George framed. Compare the standard atlas of 1890 with a modern classic – Bartholomew's *Times Atlas,* for example – and one sees what progress has been made in diagrammatic and symbolic interpretation since the 'geosopher' of Park Road launched the 'special map'.

John George's professional approach, global in all senses, raised the Edinburgh Geographical Institute above the commercial

Right: Drawing Office, Park Road 1895. Left to right: Yorston, Gunn, Purves, Elliot, Bain, McVicar, Hardie, Rennie, Mackie, Anderson, Beveridge. Friedrich Bosse's room is at the far end

Below: The Edinburgh Geographical Institute, Park Road 1889-1911

level. It became an institution, members of the *Challenger* Commission were to be found there, doyens of the arts and sciences consulted its head and were consulted by him. He corresponded with the learned societies of Paris, St Petersburg, Budapest and Chicago. (Chicago awarded him the Helen Culver Gold Medal.)

From the beginning of his career he had had two large non-commercial aims: to see a Royal Scottish Geographical Society and to see a Chair of Geography at Edinburgh University. The first was quickly realised; the second, not in his lifetime. He had to be content with seeing a lectureship established (financed and equipped largely from his own resources) and his old friend Chisholm appointed Reader.

Honours flowed to his firm and to him. Bartholomew's achieved the Grand Prix – the highest distinction – at the St Louis International Exhibition of 1904 in the United States. In 1905 John George was awarded the Victoria Gold Medal of the Royal Geographical Society for his 'successful efforts to raise the standards of cartography'. It is rare for any other than scholars or

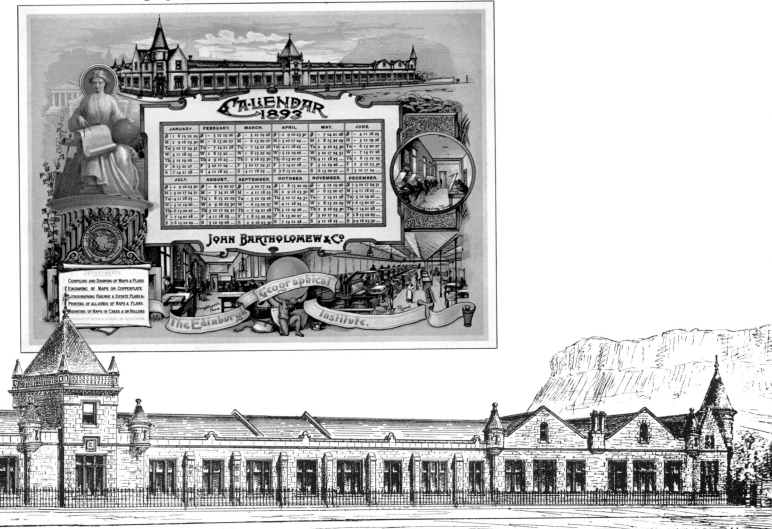

explorers to receive that award. In its centenary history, the Royal Geographical Society made particular reference to his 'enterprise in producing Atlases on a scale and of an artistic excellence not previously reached, for which . . . an appreciative public had for the first time come into existence.'

In 1909, along with J. M. Barrie the playwright, he was made Honorary Doctor of Laws of Edinburgh University and in the presentation address the Dean of the Faculty of Law called him 'a very Prince of Cartographers . . . (who) has done more than any other man to elevate and improve the standards and methods of cartographical workmanship.'

In 1910 he was appointed Geographer and Cartographer to the reigning monarch, a title which lapsed on the death of his son fifty-two years later.

John George in middle age, thin-faced and hollow-eyed, conducting much of his business from the sick-bed, found time to remove the firm in 1911 to its present handsome premises in Duncan Street on the south side of Edinburgh. (Thomas Nelson had died in 1892. John George had then taken his cousin Andrew Scott into partnership. The partnership was to last until just after the first World War, when the firm got its modern name: John Bartholomew & Son, Limited.)

The Edinburgh Geographical Institute, Duncan Street under construction with engraving of Duncan Street behind

THE EDINBURGH GEOGRAPHICAL INST

JOHN BARTHOLOMEW & CO.

Bartholomew's at last had a self-contained home of their own, a building of severe classical outline and imposing facade, appropriate to its title of Edinburgh Geographical Institute. (It was an excellent investment, but the premium was high: the new building, including the site but not the machinery or necessary alterations, cost £14,600. In those Edwardian days one might have bought a long street full of three-storied terraced houses for the same amount.)

Gilding the lily, John George had the mini-Palladian porch of Falcon Hall, a house he had earlier vacated, transported to the front of the new building; and in that respect his aesthetic judgment was, as usual, impeccable. He went to live close at hand, in Newington House. Neither Newington nor Falcon Hall have survived. The latter's lodge-gates decorate the main entrance of the Edinburgh Zoological Gardens.

Despite deteriorating health, he controlled the preparation and production of millions of military maps for the theatres of the 1914-18 war. He lost a son in that war. The elder of two surviving sons – 'Captain Ian', as employees called him – came home to

Below: Falcon Hall gates removed in 1909 and recreated at the Scottish Zoological Park in Corstorphine

Bottom: Falcon Hall, Morningside (built in 1780 by Lord Provost Coulter) and lived in by John George Bartholomew 1898-1907

understudy his father and succeed him as managing director in 1920.

To the end, John George's brain was alive with schemes. Announcing the formation of a limited company in January 1919, he told the staff that in future they would participate in the profits of the business. He presented partnership certificates to everyone, male and female, valued according to length of service and efficiency. It was a vision of the worker participation schemes that were to come before workers and employers fifty years later – but at the time some Edinburgh lawyers and businessmen must have thought John George had gone off his head.

This co-partnership scheme lasted for ten years until, at the end of 1929, the Directors felt that the money applied thereto would be better appreciated if it were received in the form of a regular extra payment of wages. Most employees took up this option but six senior staff members remained in the scheme until it finally lapsed in 1935.

In 1930, the Directors considered as a replacement, the introduction of a Savings and Pensions Scheme to which the firm would contribute. In fact it was not until 1952 that the existing Government – approved Pensions and Life Insurance Scheme was started.

By 1920 the firm was back to peacetime production and the men home from the war – but not all. William Forsyth, Allister Mitchell, Thomas Smith (all engravers) and Robert Morrison and John Robertson (litho writers) constitute the Roll of Honour of 1914-18.

'Captain Ian's' return was none too soon. Within a few months John George was himself on a voyage of discovery. Better health was his quest, but in the mountains behind Estoril, Portugal, he failed to find it.

Tributes appeared in many countries. Letters of condolence came in from distant corners of the world. An old friend, Jules de Schokalsky, president of the Geographical Society of Russia (of which John George had been a corresponding member) managed to write, though since they had last met St Petersburg had become Petrograd and life was hazardous for the Tsarist old guard.

'He was,' General de Schokalsky wrote, 'the personified truth itself, and at the same time with such goodness and unselfishness as charmed anyone who approached him. . . . Coming myself from a not cold-blooded race, I have no shame when in writing this my eyes are full of tears.'

4 Memorable Maps

There were to have been seven pillars of cartographical wisdom in the memorials of John George's time – seven magnificent volumes comprising Bartholomew's *Physical Atlas* ('Illustrating the Natural Phenomena of the Earth').★

They were his own cherished labour, to which he had recruited a formidable army of collaborators – the biggest names in the physical sciences in the British Isles, the leading specialists in their own fields in the United States, India and Australia. The work probed areas of knowledge new to map-makers. You could read in the prospectus of Storm Tracks and Frequency, Distribution of Medicinal Plants, Distribution of Domestic Animals and Parasites, Distribution of Christian Missions, the Clothing of Man, the Population of the Seas, the Comets and Meteors and many another strange topic, set forth with John George's customary diagrammatic ingenuity: an expression and fulfilment of the philosophy of one who had written, in the inaugural number of the *Scottish Geographical Magazine,* that 'maps and atlases may be said to be the epitomised record of our earth-knowledge and, in their evolution, ought to reflect the progress of civilisation.'

It was conceived as a work of Teutonic thoroughness. The solid scholarship of the German cartographers – von Stülpnagel, Augustus Petermann, Berghaus, Vogel and others – had always appealed to John George.

'The Briton's concept of geography,' he wrote, 'is essentially practical and commercial, he has an idea that trade will follow the Union Jack . . . . But the German studies geography mainly for its own sake and for the knowledge and culture it brings him . . . . The German wishes scientific maps, and he gets them . . . . To produce a scientific atlas in England is to embark on a daring philanthropic enterprise . . . . One map (to the Briton) is as good as another, possibly better, if brightly coloured . . . . In Germany, everything is different; there we have a critical appreciation of merit in all its details – projection, uniform scales, physical relief, systematic treatment, accuracy and technical excellence . . . .

> 'One may say with some truth that, if the Germans are conservative in politics, they are liberal in the arts and sciences, for an educated aristocracy rules in Germany. If the British are liberal in politics, they are conservative in science, for a half-educated democracy rules the British Empire . . . .'

(John George's father had studied with Petermann. His own son John had been in Leipzig, 1907-8, learning from the master Oswald Winkel. And he would surely have approved the journey of his grandson, another John, to Berne and Zurich in 1960 to sit at the feet of Edouard Imhof, a great Swiss cartographer who perpetuated the German tradition.)

As things turned out, the grand *Physical Atlas* never came to

★ I, Geology; II, Orography, Hydrography, Oceanography; III, Meteorology; IV, Botany; V, Zoogeography; VI, Ethnography, Demography; VII, Cosmography, Terrestrial Magnetism (refer to p90)

fruition. The scale of the project was too immense; life too short. Only two volumes appeared: *Meteorology* in 1899 and *Zoogeography* (the animal kingdom) in 1911. Expensively produced, impressively coloured, they were by no means over-priced at £2 12s 6d each.

At the other end of the spectrum, and at a price of 2s 6d, came the striking microcosm of Bartholomew's *Miniature Atlas and Gazetteer* (1894), packing 128 plates and 10,000 place-names into a compact book which fitted comfortably in one's waistcoat pocket.

The publications of John George's era, 1890 to 1920, are so numerous that one can hardly catalogue them all, yet so important, and revealing so rapid an evolution in the cartographical art, that it seems almost an insult to the directors, management and employees of those days to leave any out.★

In popular taste, nothing surpassed the Half-inch series of

★ See Appendix III for list of publications

46

general purpose maps, two miles to the inch, in which contour colouring had first been introduced. John George's father had launched No. 1, Edinburgh District. John George had issued the last of the complete series in 1903 – an achievement which Mrs Bartholomew had celebrated by giving a dinner for the heads of departments. John George's son, 'Captain Ian' (whom we shall from now on call by his proper name, John), would revise the coverage of the maps and integrate Scotland, England and Wales in one comprehensive series which would remain unchanged in its layout until the 1970s.

Most people who have had occasion to use only one map of any part of Great Britain in their lives have used one of Bartholomew's Half-inch. They are the most familiar folding maps of all time, with their dark or light blue covers and red lettering and the royal arms above. They have sold by the million, down to the present day.

It was not the fashion of John George's era to oversell with superlatives and extravagant claims – at least, it was not *his* fashion. In 1891, when he announced 'a really perfect Plan of the City of Edinburgh, engraved in minute and exact detail', he meant virtually that. It was based on a recent Ordnance survey on the gigantic scale of five feet to one mile. Bartholomew's brought this down to manageable size, fifteen inches to the mile. Today, when printing and publishing techniques are so much improved, the Edinburgh City Plan of 1891 continues to attract the wondering attention of people in the map business. You concentrate on one corner of it with a magnifying glass – which you don't really need. Every tree and bush in Greyfriars churchyard is delineated with

absolute clarity. Every lamp-post is dotted in on every pavement. So are the flower-beds in the gardens, the garden sheds, the stairways and steps of the courts and closes. There is scarcely a bracket on the wall of a wynd which has not been frozen for posterity on that plan, and the reproduction does not stop, as most reproductions do, at the outsides of the buildings. You may trace the seating arrangements in the Surgeons' Hall, count the stalls in the Court of Session, measure the curves of the benches in University lecture-rooms and study the layout of the display cases in the Science Museum.

Coloured, the sheet cost 30s. Mounted on cloth it was 45s. If you bought a mounted copy, Bartholomew's would colour and identify your own house or place of business on it, at no extra cost.

Bartholomew's Large Plan of Edinburgh & Leith

Left and Opposite: Bartholomew's New Large Plan of Edinburgh & Leith (15 inches to the mile) 1891

A new educational work by Bartholomew, published by Macmillan, came out also in 1891. It was the *Physical and Political Atlas,* containing eighty large and lavishly-detailed maps, the fruit of Bartholomew experience in that busy and fertile field. 'Too elaborate for the schoolboy,' was the only serious criticism offered when it appeared – an objection which an anonymous reviewer in the *Manchester Examiner* smartly dealt with:

'The barren committal to memory of lists of names and figures must give way to an intelligent study of maps and charts . . . . If geography is to be taught at all successfully in schools, in order to be of any practical use, it can only be by getting the pupil diligently to handle such maps as Mr Bartholomew offers . . . . To no individual worker is to be attributed the progress (in atlas design) more than to Mr J. G. Bartholomew.'

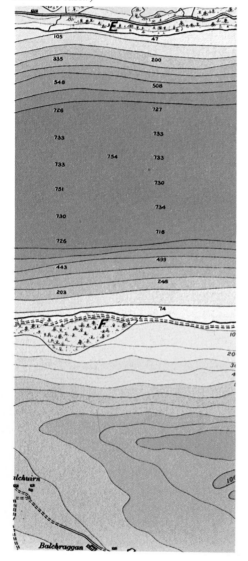

A section of Loch Ness (surveyed in 1904) prepared for Murray's Bathymetrical Survey of the Scottish Fresh-Water Lochs 1910. (Maximum depth 754 ft – where monsters lurk?)

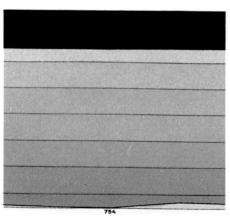

The large and costly (£3 3s.) *Survey Atlas of Scotland,* put out in 1894 under the auspices of the Royal Scottish Geographical Society, placed that country well ahead in the matter of summaries and illustrations of recent Ordnance findings, of the Admiralty and Geological Surveys and of the most up-to-date meteorological, archaeological and natural history studies. Notable scholars occupied University chairs at that period: Sir Archibald Geikie and his brother James – J. A. Harvie-Brown – George Adam Smith – Alexander Buchan of the warm and cold spells. All were friends and advisers of John George.

The atlas hinted at the social and economic changes which were coming over Scotland. Reduced in prominence were the old parish churches and gentlemen's seats. Arrived were post-offices and railway stations, hotels and inns, classification of roads by colour, rights of way and footpaths, viaducts, cuttings and embankments and steamer routes. The sporting laird still found a page devoted to deer forests and salmon rivers.

In 1904 Bartholomew's brought out a third edition of the *Survey Gazetteer of the British Isles,* modernised from the 1901 census and the latest topographical and commercial returns. At a price of 17s 6d it offered a full range of maps at ten miles to the inch, with fifteen town plans and a collection of specialist maps looking into such hitherto-uncharted regions as the Death Rate from Zymotic Diseases, Lunacy and Pauperism, Green and Corn Crops, Hardware Manufacturers, and Protestants and Roman Catholics in Ireland. The gazetteer section answered, for every inhabited spot and natural curiosity in the British Isles, the two questions which every student – John George had said – must ask: "Where is it?" and "What about it?"

In the Edwardian era, John George acknowledged an expanding economy with his *Grand Atlas of the World's Commerce* ('The Whole Fiscal Question Clearly Illustrated'). It came out in twenty-two sixpenny parts originally, with allegorical frontispiece depicting an Atlantic liner, an express freight train, Britannia with trident, shield and cornucopia, and plenty of sunbeams.

Some of the most beautiful maps ever seen were included in the *Bathymetric Survey of Scottish Freshwater Lochs* of 1910, the water depths being indicated by gradations of pure blues. In this work John George had the aid of Sir John Murray of *Challenger* fame. (It was Sir John, during his oceanographic surveys in the Pacific, who named the 25,000-foot trench off Antofagasta, Chile, the 'Bartholomew Deep' in honour of his friend.)

The bathymetric maps look good today, and the fact that they exist has had some influence in 1976 on the Ordnance Survey's decision to mark the water depths in its new survey of Great Britain on the metric scale (1 : 50000).

Nineteen-twelve saw the publication of the *Citizen's Atlas,* a new large edition of a work first issued in 1898, when it sold 141,000 copies. For 25s the citizen was put in possession of 156 stoutly-bound, big pages of coloured maps. The *Daily Express* had

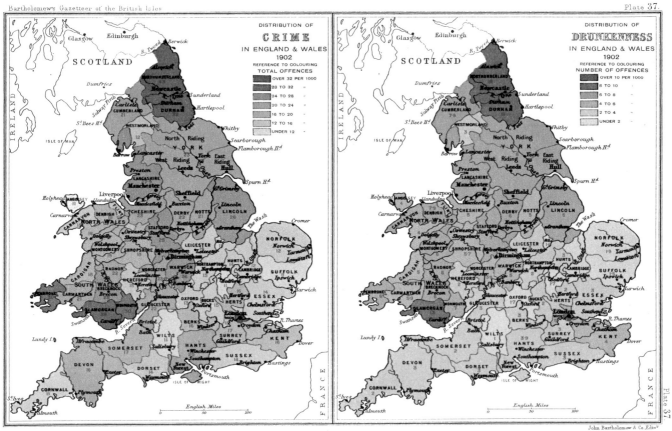

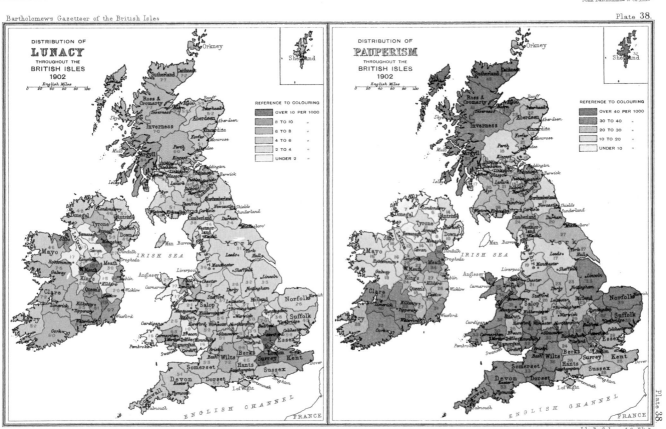

Early thematic maps on a social theme produced for the Gazetteer of the British Isles 1904 edition

no hesitation in calling it 'the very best atlas which can be purchased at the price.' The *Scotsman* was equally enthusiastic:

'The richly-detailed material of these plates is brought well into hand . . . by an index so extraordinarily full that only long-continued use could adequately test its utility.'

The *Daily Chronicle's* admiration was so warmly expressed that it must have softened the irritation of Doctor Bartholomew – a Scot of Scots – on reading that his atlas reflected 'high credit on English topography.'

'Indispensable during the War' was the publisher's claim for the *International Reference Atlas of the World,* published in 1914, price 10s 6d. It included an introductory essay, an index of 25,000 place-names and a key to pronunciations. Bartholomew's were by that date settled in at their spacious Duncan Street factory and were filling it up with new machinery. 'Revolutionary production methods,' the advertisement said, 'have enabled us to halve the old prices without sacrificing accuracy or quality.'

If the first decade and a half was a heroic age of cartography, it was also a happy time for map buyers. Books and maps would never be so cheap again – nor of such high quality, some said. The time had arrived when any man who aspired to a shelf of books had to have an atlas on it; and when energetic folk, attracted by the pocket folding maps, actually went walking, riding and driving for the pleasure of comparing the state of the map with the state of the ground. Addressing the Royal Geographical Society, Rudyard Kipling said:

"As soon as men begin to talk about anything that really matters, *someone has to go and get the atlas"* – and *the* atlas was almost inevitably a Bartholomew atlas.

The war of 1914-18 transformed the Edinburgh Geographical Institute into a factory for war maps and an auxiliary of the government cartographical departments, but prestige projects were not all lost sight of or put in cold storage. In 1915 there came a remarkable production, the *Atlas of the Holy Land,* price 25s. It was designed and edited by Professor George Adam Smith of Aberdeen University and supervised by Doctor Bartholomew personally. More than twenty years had gone by since those two old friends first planned the work. Illness, separation and pressures of other business had forced it time and again to the back of the queue, but it had been a labour of love, to which each had escaped whenever he could spare the time. The result was an astonishing compendium of religious history. In the purely geographical treatment of the Holy Land, the scale was four miles to the inch – larger than the official government surveys of most foreign countries were at that period able to offer.

As Professor Adam Smith pointed out, Israel's political geography was not the easiest subject for a scholar to master or a cartographer to delineate. In a series of related maps there must be shown the stormy history of that land over thirty or forty centuries – the foreign conquests, the frequent alterations in administration, the fragmentations of the kingdoms, the oscillations of the frontiers, Israelite uprisings against oppressors, the rise and fall of petty tyrants, the history of the free cities (of which large-scale street plans were provided).

The *Atlas of the Holy Land* dealt with pre-Biblical trade routes, the expansion of Rome, the journeys of the apostles and the Crusades – every event of Middle Eastern history and everything that went to make up the history of a Christian country of the West, complicated for the geographer by a setting where not even the physical features of the landscape had remained constant, where tribal confines had varied from year to year and the identification of ancient place-names with modern was still something which archaeologists and historians acrimoniously argued about.

It might have been a digest of the many Bible atlases already in print, but that was not John George's way. It emerged unique, owing nothing to what had gone before, an excellent example of the selective thoroughness and artistic refinement which John George preached, and the accurate up-to-date treatment which had come to be associated with his name.

For fifteen years, preliminary work on the most renowned of map books, *The Times Survey Atlas,* had been in his hands. It would contain a hundred large and elaborate plates. There would be an index of 200,000 items. No expense would be spared to make it the one atlas which scholars, libraries and institutions could not afford to be without. One bound copy would weigh eighteen and three-quarter pounds, and the print order would be 60,000 – the crazed tiling of Duncan Street's entrance hall, where they had to store some of the paper for it, is a memento of the awesome weight of that enterprise. For Doctor Bartholomew it would be (a descendant says) 'the culmination of his life's work as a dedicated scientist and geographer.' All but ready for the press when the first World War ended, *The Times Atlas* was published in 1922, two years after his death.

Ptolemy World Map from The Times Atlas

5 Work & Play

In the oak-panelled room on Duncan Street, lined with old globes, two worlds – learning and adventuring – met and conferred. Discovery fertilised science. Along the corridor a hundred or so employees of the Edinburgh Geographical Institute – draughtsmen, engravers, printers, patchers, tinters, clerks, apprentices and warehousemen – performed tasks which looked glamorous enough to the outsider but in reality were often tedious and repetitive.

Like cartographical engravers, cartographical draughtsmen were the élite of their craft and the backbone of the business. The diary of James Bain opens a window on the small world of a Bartholomew draughtsman about the turn of the century. And it gives some idea of the quality of the man John George employed.

Bain joined as an apprentice in 1888 and ended his career as managing editor of the London firm of Geographia. His friend Hardie, 'a very clever boy and most ambitious'*, started off on the wrong foot, for he passed a Civil Service examination during the first year of his apprenticeship and the firm refused to release him. 'Hardie brought in the sum of his indenture and laid it on the manager's desk and this so angered Mr Bartholomew that he had his Civil Service appointment cancelled' – but Hardie eventually won his way into the Admiralty and was seen on board the fleet flagship at Constantinople in 1918, representing the Hydrographer of the Navy at the Turkish surrender.

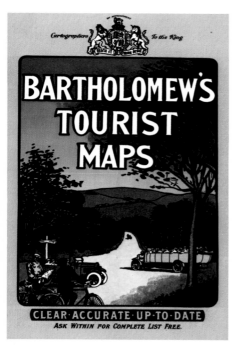

Tennant, another contemporary of Bain's, became the General Post Office's chief draughtsman. Another boy went to the *Daily Mail* as its map drawer. Two Bartholomew-trained youths of the same vintage rose to very senior positions in the Ordnance Survey at Southampton and later on there were ex-Bartholomew boys in the posts of Surveyor-General in Bengal and South Africa.

Before World War I a number of employees emigrated to Canada. Some returned, others stayed on and did well. One of them, George Aitken, rose to be Surveyor-General of British Columbia. Two who chose the United States in the same period made important careers for themselves: John Philip in the American Geographical Society, Charles Riddiford in the National Geographic Society.

A few weeks before this book was published, there died in Scotland one of the most remarkable of Bartholomew draughtsmen. William Logan, crippled and legless from an early age, self-educated, went to the Survey of Egypt in 1912 (where he taught himself Arabic), became superintendent of the drawing office and produced the maps which Lawrence of Arabia used in his desert exploits. Logan received the M.B.E.

John Moir, draughtsman, was appointed Assistant Surveyor-General of Malaya and after that country's independence he returned to his *alma mater* in Duncan Street, to be drawing office foreman. Even the Bartholomew warehouseman went on retirement to be superintendent of the Edinburgh Public Swimming Baths.

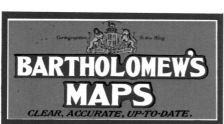

* Quotations in this chapter are taken from the manuscript diary of James Bain

A Bartholomew apprentice found he had bound himself to a life of considerable prestige but hard labour, strict discipline and low pay. Bain started at a shilling a week, aged sixteen, and was taken on at £1 a week when he came out of his time at twenty-one. Thereafter his pay went up by a shilling per week per annum. Despite poverty, Bartholomew apprentices could give themselves airs among the employees of less distinguished houses. It was an apprentice jibe in Edinburgh that when Bartholomew boys went for another job they turned up for interview in frock coats and top hats. Some of them actually did.

Occasionally the tedium of routine work became almost insupportable. 'Some time in the early nineties,' Bain recalls,

> 'Mr Bartholomew decided to increase the number of contours on the Half-inch Scotland and I was given the job to prepare the copy for the engravers . . . . When a sufficient amount of copy was ready, the engravers' apprentices were put on the job of engraving the new contours in fine dots on the copper plates. This led to the only bit of labour trouble Bartholomew's ever had, as far as I ever heard. The contour work was very monotonous and, though necessary, could hardly be said to be useful to the lads in learning their trade. And so after a time they went on strike . . . . Mr Bartholomew was very annoyed about this and took pretty strong measures, I believe, but I don't remember what was done . . . .'

(John George, stern and silent, was 'a saintly old man' to workmen who knew him well; to others, and to the youngsters, he was a holy terror.)

John George, and more especially his hospitable wife, were punctilious in maintaining *esprit* and good relations at the Edinburgh Geographical Institute. In spite of his poor health, the 'owner' presided over regular parties and pleasure trips and sometimes he had the senior craftsmen to supper at his house in Blacket Place, a stone's-throw from Duncan Street. James Bain was there the evening Doctor Hugh Robert Mill the meteorologist and several other University lecturers arrived. 'He and Mr Bartholomew and some other gentlemen were talking together when I heard Doctor Mill raise the old question: *"What is the meaning of the words in the song, You'll tak' the high road and I'll tak' the low?"* I don't know if they settled the vexed question.'

Mrs Bartholomew dined heads of departments on great occasions in the firm's history, such as the completion of an important atlas or map series; and she organised the Annual Picnic, the central event of the summer season, on which conversations and clothes budgets were concentrated for weeks beforehand and afterwards. As the date drew near, practice for the sports became more frenetic and collisions in the long corridor between offices and printing room – the amateur athletes' sprinting track – more frequent.

The Picnic took place either at the Carlops (south of Edinburgh, three hours by wagonette) or at some stately home of the Lothians. There the employees travelled in four-in-hand coaches, brilliantly decked out and drawn by beribboned horses. One year it was at Arniston, a house of the Dundas family (the

name of whose viscountcy, Melville, appears on so many maps).
James Bain: 'Swings for our use were fixed up on the trees and
there were cricket pitches. Unlimited quantities of hot water for tea
were provided and there were oceans of milk and in fact everything
was done to help us enjoy ourselves.'

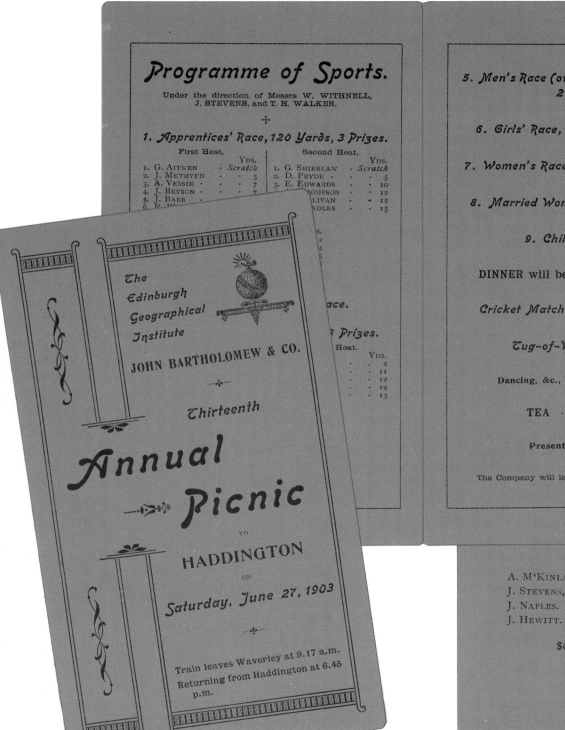

Programme of Sports.

Under the direction of Messrs W. WITHNELL,
J. STEVENS, and T. H. WALKER.

✠

1. Apprentices' Race, 120 Yards, 3 Prizes.

First Heat.	YDS.	Second Heat.	YDS.
1. G. AITKEN	Scratch	1. G. SHIERLAW	Scratch
2. J. METHVEN	5	2. D. PRYDE	5
3. A. VESSIE	7	3. E. EDWARDS	10
4. J. BRYSON	7	THOMPSON	12
5. J. BARR		LIVAN	12
6.		NDLES	15

5. Men's Race (over 40 years), 80 Yards.
2 Prizes.

✠

6. Girls' Race, 80 Yards. 3 Prizes.

✠

7. Women's Race, 80 Yards. 2 Prizes.

✠

8. Married Women's Race. 2 Prizes.

✠

9. Children's Races.

✠

DINNER will be served at 12.30 p.m.

✠

Cricket Match—Married v. Single.

✠

Tug-of-War—5-a-Side.

✠

Dancing, &c., during the Afternoon.

✠

TEA · · · 4 p.m.

✠

Presentation of Prizes.

✠

The Company will leave for the Station at 6 p.m.

The
Edinburgh
Geographical
Institute

JOHN BARTHOLOMEW & CO.

Thirteenth

Annual Picnic

TO

HADDINGTON

ON

Saturday, June 27, 1903

Train leaves Waverley at 9.17 a.m.
Returning from Haddington at 6.45
p.m.

Committee.

A. M'KINLAY.	W. COCKBURN.
J. STEVENS, Junr.	T. H. WALKER.
J. NAPLES.	J. METHVEN.
J. HEWITT.	W. WITHNELL.

Secretary and Convener.

W. WITHNELL.

In winter came the Annual Soirée, Concert and Dance, when all the talents of draughtsmen, colourists and printers were harnessed to the production of programmes. We have Bain's copy of the card for the Fourth Annual Soirée, 'J. G. Bartholomew Esq. in the Chair':

Song, *The Admiral's Broom*   Mr Fotheringham
Song, *The Dear Homeland*   Miss McEwing
Indian Club Exhibition   Mr Annan
Reading, *Up in a Balloon*   Mr Foote

– and so on, a charming souvenir of the kind of evening few can now have memories of, when hard-working men and women competed cheerfully to entertain each other and never thought of hiring a professional singer or musician.

EDINBURGH GEOGRAPHICAL INSTITUTE

ALBYN ROOMS
THURSDAY, 29TH DECEMBER 1921
7.30 P.M.

The first World War seemed to annihilate all the spontaneous gaiety of ordinary people. Things were never quite the same again, though at the annual Supper Dance which superseded both Picnic and Soirée it is recalled that 'there was always entertainment from the more talented guests in the way of songs, violin solos etc.'

Company outings to Rothesay, the Trossachs, the Border country and other places were until recently a feature of the summer season but, in 1976, of all the social whirl of the past, only the Supper Dance survives. The firm's once-formidable Bowling

Golf Outing, West Linton, June 1934
Left to Right:
Kenneth Cousland
George Robinson
Jock Davidson
Fred Porteous
Bob Trotter
Alex Duff
Cliff Kerr
Andrew Aikman
J.B.
Jimmy Campbell
Jimmy Park (Secretary)
Willie Dickson
George Paterson
Tom Murray
Sandy Williamson
Andrew Imrie
Francis Conacher
Jimmy Stevens

Club (it competed in the Edinburgh Printers Division) is a casualty of the modern double-shift system of work, which renders some of the team unavailable at the time of fixtures. A formerly active Photographic Club no longer exists.

The Golf Club flourishes. It is approaching its diamond jubilee and an event of its year is the foursome knock-out competition for a Rose Bowl presented by James Park, who was club secretary for many years.

The social life of the old days was therapeutic, an opportunity

to let off steam. High spirits in working hours were not wanted in the cartographic business; patience was the virtue. Bain notes that before his time the heads of geographical firms liked to get hold of crippled boys, to make them into draughtsmen – they were less inclined to fidget and wander about.

Because of his fondness for seeing what was going on in other departments, Bain was often in trouble. 'I loved seeing the printing of the maps, and when it was one I had had a hand in preparing, or one of special interest, I just had to see it in the machine.'

The drawing office personality of his time was Herr Friedrich Bosse, a German who bore an honoured cartographic name. As long ago as 1645, Abraham Bosse published a treatise on a method of transferring manuscript images to copper plates. Friedrich himself was destined for cartographical honours in Germany, but in the 1890s he was serving John George Bartholomew and studying British techniques, by courtesy of the freemasonry which existed among international cartographical firms.

Bosse by name and bossy by nature, he was not universally liked. 'In fact he was disliked,' Bain says, 'for his boasting and always comparing our work unfavourably with the German . . . . He was praising the work of some German to Dr Peach, a gentleman of the Geological Survey who used to come about the office in connection with the geological map of Scotland which was then being prepared. Dr Peach got so exasperated that when Bosse finished up his praises of this German by saying "Ach, what he had in his head!"– Dr Peach cut in: "Did he ever try a small-toothed comb?" '

Bain remembered how the *Challenger* maps 'caused quite a thrill in the department' when the Commission, which had been sitting since he was a small child, finally produced its report. The humblest Bartholomew employee felt himself involved in such great events; and there were occasions of high-level panic when he was called upon to uphold the honour of the firm:

'Lord Roberts was the central figure,' Bain remembers, on such an occasion. 'It had been arranged for him to give a lecture to the Royal Scottish Geographical Society on Russian encroachments in India. Five or six diagrams had been prepared by Bartholomew's and in case he desired any alterations or additions I·was sent to the lecture hall early in the day to carry out his wishes. When Lord Roberts arrived at the hall with Colonel Bailey, the secretary, he stormed about the diagrams, saying they weren't at all what he wanted and were useless to him.

'Colonel Bailey blamed Mr Bartholomew, but his lordship didn't want to know who was to blame but what could be done about it. It was here that I was called in. I had heard all the altercation and would, I think, have pledged the firm to anything. I was rapidly and snappily told what part of the north-west frontier and central Asia was to be shown. Then a number of place-names was rattled off and I had to write them down. A few I knew but most I didn't and just had to scribble down what I could and trust to luck, as I didn't dare ask his lordship to repeat a name or spell it. 'By the time I had got all his instructions it was lunch time and the lecture was timed for seven that evening. I rushed out of the hall and got a cab to take me to Park Road, where I created a stir with my news. Bosse, who had had a hand in preparing the original diagrams, wanted to supervise the preparation of the new ones (he was obviously annoyed that a youngster like myself should have seen Lord Roberts) but Mr Bartholomew put the job in the hands of one of the other draughtsmen with me helping. In the end I saw the diagrams hung up in the hall just as the audience was beginning to gather.'

James Bain, with a wife and family to support, left Bartholomew's and went to Philip's in London, where they paid him twice the salary and reduced his fifty-hour week to forty-six. When he could afford it, he began exploring foreign countries. Their romance and mystery had captivated him through the medium of cartographical draughtsmanship. 'I have always had the desire to wander,' he wrote. 'I have often wondered why geographical draughtsman seem to have so little desire to see the world, or even the less-frequented parts of their own country.'

Bathymetrical Chart of the Indian Ocean, from the Voyage of HMS Challenger

6 Between the Wars

An unbroken genealogy, father to son, for a century and a half is rare in the commercial world. Take Bartholomew history back to its apprentice-engraver origins and the continuity extends to close on two centuries. Yet individual Bartholomews were not long-lived. Except for George the founder's father, who died at eighty-seven (in 1871), successive heads of firm and family went at the height of their intellectual powers; and invariably their years were clouded with illness.

John senior reached fifty-six (he died in 1861); John junior sixty-two (1893); and John George, 'Prince of Cartographers', sixty (1920).

The abiding strength of the firm was the presence at every crisis of some young Bartholomew, trained and devoted to the work. From the grasp of the elder, the torch fell into capable hands.

More than once, large prosperous companies cast covetous eyes on Bartholomew's. There was the abortive attempt at a takeover by George Philip in 1879. Amalgamated Press Limited, in 1915, wanted a stake in a quality map house and made tempting offers; but they insisted on financial control, and John George would not surrender that.

Immediately after the first World War, Bartholomew's big rivals, W. & A. K. Johnston Limited, initiated long discussions about a merger. They came to nothing and, since then, Johnston's themselves have fallen.

More recently, reputable large publishing firms have several times approached Bartholomew's with a take-over bid. It has always, says the present chairman, 'been politely resisted. Our independence is important to us and, provided we can raise the necessary capital when it is required, and as shareholders we do not succumb to Government legislation, we shall preserve it. Luckily the shareholding is broadly based.'

John, the 'Captain Ian' of the first World War, took over at the Edinburgh Geographical Institute at the age of thirty. He had been at Merchiston Castle School in Edinburgh and had studied geography at Leipzig and Paris and with the German master Oswald Winkel. Returning to Edinburgh to take his arts degree, he had been under the tuition of venerable Bartholomew associates, Doctor George Chisholm and Professor James Geikie. A fellow-student remembers a class excursion over the Bathgate Hills in West Lothian, when Geikie's party got lost in the mist and John Bartholomew, the only one who had thought of bringing a whistle, rounded them all up. He was a keen climber and hill-walker, and had slept many a night in the heather.

John had joined the Army as a Territorial sergeant in August 1914 and before the year was out had been a subaltern in the Gordon Highlanders. Over the next two years, in France and Flanders, he had been three times mentioned in despatches, wounded and awarded the Military Cross. He had spent the latter half of the war (in which his brother Hugh was killed) on Haig's staff at St Omer and Montreuil, as a staff-captain of Intelligence. On demobilisation he had completed his arts course and entered the firm to understudy his ailing father. One year later he had taken control of John Bartholomew & Son, Limited.

He married Marie-Antoinette, a niece of Charles Sarolea, professor of French at Edinburgh University. Over the next few years they assured the succession by producing four sons and two daughters.

John's name is not associated with any sensational cartographical break-through. His task was to complete the unfinished projects of his father, to build on foundations his father had laid, to dictate policy and stay ahead of the times.

Business was more complex than anything his grandfather or great-grandfather could have envisaged. The problem was to keep the balance between bread-and-butter map publishing and the kind of esoteric work with which the Bartholomew name was associated – work of high academic standard, needing big capital outlay and expenditure over a long period. The one must support the other.

Map-making was more than a matter of reducing and generalising surveys into handy reference form. The Edinburgh Geographical Institute had the reputation of a research building where, side by side with demonstrations of new techniques in cartography, there had grown up an organisation for assembling and co-ordinating statistics on scientific subjects – a sort of data processing plant. When information had been sifted and checked and arranged in order for presentation in map or atlas form, men at the very top of their professions would gather with the Bartholomew of the day to sift again, and philosophise about the needs of the student or specialist for whom the plate under discussion (one of hundreds) was intended.

John fell heir to the most important job his firm had tackled, *The Times Survey Atlas*. It was to be the standard British reference atlas, a more ambitious thing altogether than *The Times* atlases brought out in 1895 and 1900. His father had worked on it until, within sight of its completion, war had broken out. The staff either went for military service or stayed for military map production. The upheavals of the next five years involved in some respects a fresh start with *The Times Atlas*.

John Bartholomew 'Ian' 1890-1962

It came out in 1922 and was hailed as the most complete and elegant work of its kind. Comparing it with the atlas of some old master of a hundred years earlier, one had a vivid picture of the progress of cartography. The old one, with its large format, engraved plates and relief shown by hachures, its sparing use of colour and its sprawling lettering and baroque flourishes, bore as much resemblance to the new example as did a stage-coach to a Rolls Royce. By a painstaking refinement of colour lithography and judicious combinations of engraving techniques, Bartholomew's had improved the content of maps and made them more appealing to the eye. Contour layer colouring, devised by John's grandfather, had marked one decisive stage. It was now in general world use; and in *The Times Atlas* it was seen in all its glory.

John George had brought about 'special maps' on subjects not formerly associated with geographers. *The Times Atlas* was a monument to his foresight. It exploited all the possibilities of 'special maps'. At the turn of the century men had looked on them with suspicion; by 1922 they were an essential feature of every respectable atlas.

The provenance of the two previous *Times* atlases had been dubious. They had 'all the signs of having been produced in Germany,' an expert said.★ But no one in the profession could doubt where the new atlas came from. As Hugh Robert Mill remarked, Bartholomew atlases and maps had a style. You recognised them at a glance, without looking for the imprint.

John Bartholomew's outstanding productions in a continuous stream of material to meet the demands of many nations and tastes were a quartet of publications universally acclaimed: the *Handy Reference Atlas;* a new *Citizen's Atlas of the World;* a *Survey Gazetteer of the British Isles;* and an *Advanced Atlas of Modern Geography*. Three were the brilliant offspring of pre-war best-sellers and the fourth broke completely new ground. They proclaimed that geography itself was advancing and mingling with the advances of other sciences. The quip that 'geography is about maps and history is about chaps' was not yet current, but it expressed an idea which had been obsolete at Bartholomew's for some time. Geography was about maps *and* chaps and much more.

Activities of the 1920s and 1930s were steady but not showy. The head of the firm himself was a diffident person, thoughtful and kindly in his own circle, cold and withdrawn with strangers. In Flanders he had contracted chronic arthritis and he suffered from it for the rest of his life. It put a stop to one of his keen pleasures, roaming the hills and glens of his homeland.

He examined his business and its future. Work studies, management consultants and efficiency experts had not been heard of; it was for Bartholomew himself to streamline and mechanise, improve printing methods, experiment with styles of lettering to suit modern tastes and ensure that maps kept their clarity and

★ Gerald R. Crone, Keeper of Maps at the Royal Geographical Society in London

accuracy in a world of faster pace and increasingly lax standards.

In Duncan Street he installed printing presses of the new rotary off-set type. (The old hand-fed machines, known as flat-beds, had printed off a lithographic stone at a few hundred impressions per hour. The rotary presses introduced in the early 1900s had transferred impressions direct from plate to paper at three or four times that rate. The new off-set press, transferring its impressions by way of a rubber blanket, could print several colours in rapid succession at a speed of 7,000 sheets per hour or faster – though at Bartholomew's, to preserve high definition, they kept it down to 5,000.)

The search for perfection led into technological labyrinths and great expense. The fittings of colours and print to their shapes became so critical that something had to be done about the effects of atmospheric change on the tension of the paper. John Bartholomew put in an air-conditioning plant. Air-conditioning requires a water supply, and he sank a well in the basement of the building. How far down were they? Any traces of dampness yet? – present-day Bartholomews recall from childhood the excitements and disappointments of that calculated risk. Water in the necessary quantities was found at four hundred feet. The same well still supplies the air-conditioning plant, and temperature and humidity have been controlled to this day.

Towards the 1930s, photo-lithography was the coming thing. Followed by photo-composition, photo-colouring and the 'stripping-in' of lettering, it accelerated the preparation of coloured material at no sacrifice of accuracy. The 42″ x 32″ camera which John Bartholomew mounted in his works in 1928 was the biggest of its type in Scotland. Two years later he launched the first Bartholomew atlas to have all its colours photographically made up.

The head of the firm became, like his father, a pillar of the Scottish establishment. He devoted money and energy, as his father had done, to the improvement of geography teaching in Edinburgh. The university lectureship became a chair, and Alan Ogilvie its professor. From 1920 John was honorary secretary of the Royal Scottish Geographical Society, a post left vacant at his father's death. (Thirty years on, when he became the Society's vice-president, he handed on the honorary secretaryship to his own son John.) In 1953 he was president of the Royal Scottish Geographical Society; one of his early duties was to make the formal announcement of the conquest of Everest by a British expedition.

He served on the Permanent Committee for Geographical Names – a body of wise men which agrees policies, definitive spellings for place-names and settles various other editorial and cartographical ambiguities. John Bartholomew's firm was the first to adopt the committee's recommendations, and his son John succeeded him as a member.

'His ever-active mind,' an old colleague, Dr Douglas Allan,* has written, 'was always seeking further advances towards

* President of the Royal Scottish Geographical Society and Director of the Royal Scottish Museum

65

perfection . . . . New methods of map projection, cleaner colours for differentiation, better type for lettering and paper more resistant to variations in temperature . . . . the Edinburgh Geographical Institute in his time was a laboratory to which students came for instruction and experimentation.'

In 1956 his old university made him a Doctor of Laws. In 1960 he was appointed C.B.E. and in 1961 the Royal Geographical Society bestowed on him the rare distinction of a Founder's Medal – an honour which took into account the services to cartography of the house of Bartholomew down the ages.

To satisfy one public demand with a map or atlas was to create another need. Hard on the heels of the motor-car era came the era of flight, giving rise to new orientations of maps. (The problems which beset the old map-makers, of representing hills and valleys on a flat surface, were trivial compared with the problems which had to be solved when you represented the earth's curvature two-dimensionally.) On 11th January 1949 the *Scotsman* quoted John Bartholomew at a meeting of the Royal Society of Edinburgh:

'Maps of the world will have to be projected with their centres nearer the North Pole, affording better directional properties for flying and other modern requirements. That is why I favour the new system of oblique projection which I have proposed.
'The new projections are "Atlantis", a transverse, oblique, homolographic projection; "Regional", an irregular development of the conic, with two standard parallels; and "Nordic", an oblique application of "Aitoff".'

A practical illustration of what John Bartholomew was getting at may be seen when you sit in an aircraft and study the small booklet of maps which you find in the seat-pocket in front of you. Many international airlines have adopted Bartholomew projections.

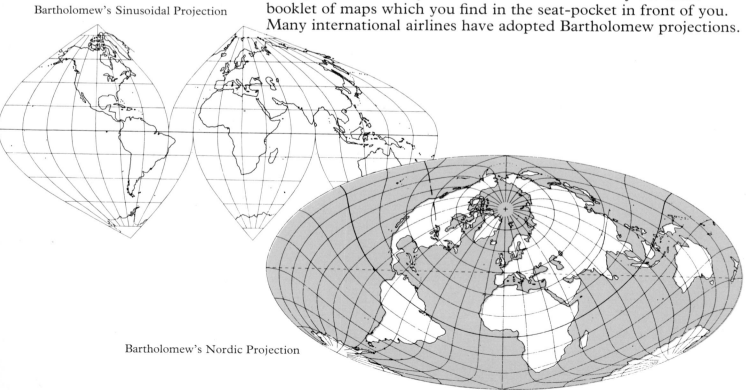

Bartholomew's Sinusoidal Projection

Bartholomew's Nordic Projection

7 Towards Perfection

For the 140 employees of the firm the second World War was like the first, only more so. Modern military planning, logistics and all the staff-work inherent in a global strategy and mobile tactics demanded maps and plans in quantities, and at speeds, hitherto undreamed-of. (During the swift Allied advance through Normandy in 1944, Bartholomew's found themselves printing maps for forward areas which Montgomery's Army had already left behind.)

The disruption of map production in the south of England through air raids brought extra worries. When the Ordnance Survey headquarters at Southampton was obliterated and large map stocks lost, Bartholomew's knew they would not lack business as long as the war lasted – and that was a blessing, since it filled the gap created when the Control of Maps Order 1940 restricted, for security reasons, the production and sale of maps above a certain scale.

Through bombing, Bartholomew's lost their London office. It had been opened in 1934 at 66 Chandos Place, W.C.2, with Francis Robinson, son of one of the firm's directors, in charge. It has not been replaced. Bartholomew's find that air travel makes contact with the capital easy and that customers like to visit the historic building in Edinburgh and confer with resident experts.

One of the firm's wartime souvenirs is a map of Germany, fully detailed and printed on silk. Spread out, it is the size of a large handkerchief. Crushed up, it can be hidden in jacket pocket or lining. Bartholomew's supplied it for the use of airmen and others who ran the risk of finding themselves fugitives in enemy territory.

Enlistment and call-up depleted the staff. John and Peter, sons of the head of the firm, were in the Army in their teens, John surveying with the Royal Engineers in the Middle East, Peter a subaltern in the Scots Guards, wearing (as his father had done) the Military Cross. Peter ended the war a major.

Robert, the third son, only eighteen when the war ended, went into the Gordon Highlanders and served in Malaya and in 1948 he entered the firm.

Flying Officer Victor Pidot of the office staff was killed in action in March 1944.

Two members of the firm, William Dickson and James Park, received the M.B.E. for their contributions to the war effort.

After world conflict, empires crumbled, nations were split up, populations migrated and new and unfamiliar names replaced old and cherished ones all over the globe. Cartographers were kept busy recording these changes – not always dispassionately. John Bartholomew supported Mr Winston Churchill in deploring Persia's decision to alter its name to Iran – 'a new-fangled name coined by an upstart sovereign to justify his own conceited ideas,' he said.

Diagrammatically and pictorially the map-makers documented the results of cataclysmic change, and a fresh generation of

Letter from Winston Churchill

10, Downing Street,
Whitehall.

19th November, 1954

Dear Mr. Bartholomew,

Thank you so much for sending me a copy of "The Edinburgh World Atlas". It was most kind of you, and I am very pleased to accept it.

Yours sincerely,

Winston S. Churchill

John Bartholomew, Esq., M.C., F.R.G.S.

Bartholomews (the sixth) came into the firm when the three sons, John, Peter and Robert, completed their military service and their studies.

Post-war years brought increased business from a world which had been starved of the cartographical material it had learned to rely on. The appetites of motoring and tourist organisations and shipping lines, the airlines and youth hostel associations, needed large print orders to satisfy them. A hungry public devoured the *Road Atlas of Great Britain* (brought out in 1943), the *Compact Atlas* (1943) and the *Regional Atlas* (1948) as soon as these works were available in unlimited quantities.

A sign of the post-war times was the phenomenon of a comparatively insignificant change in public taste or advertising emphasis provoking chaos in business – half the staff laid off, or all the staff on overtime, through the whim of someone on the other side of the world, perhaps. An example was the giveaway map gimmick, promoted by United States petrol companies. It quickly spread to Britain. From the early 1950s Bartholomew's turned out giveaway and subsidised maps by the hundred thousand – a satisfactory short-term assignment, but against it had to be weighed the danger that motorists might grow out of the habit of buying their own maps.

Nine educational atlases, revised and updated, were still coming off the presses. Special school editions were done for Australia, Canada, South Africa and India. (The Indian atlases appeared in six different languages: Bengali, Hindi, Marathi, Tamil, Telugu and Urdu.)

Scribing Tools

In 1953 and 1954 came the important *Columbus Atlas* and *Edinburgh World Atlas* and the following year the globe of John Bartholomew's career spun full circle. He took on the new *Times Atlas*. The previous edition had crowned his father's achievements; this one – to be known as the 'Mid-century Edition'– was to crown his. It was to be as definitive a work as the latest mechanical aids and the accumulated wisdom of the Edinburgh Geographical Institute could make it. It was to comprise five volumes and to occupy five of the last seven years of his life (1955-1960).

Characteristically he redesigned all his plates to give a regional covering more in tune with the age. He disposed of a small criticism of contour layer colouring by introducing new symbols for particular landforms – escarpments, for instance, where the colours did not always convey the true impression. Coated plastic sheets came in to join the metal plates and lithographic stones and to inaugurate, with custom-built tools, the new technique of 'scribing'.

For some lettering he used the 'blue plate' instead of the black. They were all minor changes to those who would only sub-consciously appreciate the results, but to a cartographer they represented historic improvements.

'There can be no higher praise for an atlas,' said the *Observer* when Volume III, first of the five to be published, came out, 'than

to say it combines comprehensiveness with clarity. These are indeed the most striking qualities of the *Times Atlas of the World*, edited by John Bartholomew . . . . The type used for the geographical names and the colouring of the maps are chosen with ingenuity and taste, the material incorporated is vast without being confusing, so that with the help of the excellent index even the smallest place can be found easily and without strain to the eye. It is a beautiful production, outstanding as a source of up-to-date geographical information.'

Its compiler's friends noted a personal touch: John Bartholomew had paid a tribute to his old master Oswald Winkel by including a section of maps on Winkel's 'tripel' projection.

The perfect atlas? The cartographer would say there can be no such thing. Perfection is something to strive for, never to attain. As the Bartholomew chairman has said,★ "Nothing goes out of date more quickly than a map." Somewhere in the world something is going on which will render every new map old-fashioned in some tiny respect as it rolls off the press.

The *Times Atlas* was produced in circumstances not the most favourable for acquiring or checking information. In Europe, the cold war was on, the iron curtain was firmly drawn across half the continent. "There was a cartographical curtain, at any rate," John recalled in a newspaper interview. But he was able to carry out reliable small-scale mapping of the socialist lands with the aid of the Soviet *Atlas Mira,* which was published in 1954. China after the revolution proved more difficult. The Bartholomew intelligence network was severely taxed, but eventually it found 'referees' for the facts and figures of almost every country in the world. The local knowledge supplied by correspondents in remote places, some of them trapped under hostile regimes, permitted the inclusion of many significant features and developments which would otherwise have been missed.

Reviewers found the *Times Atlas* (at five guineas a volume) amazingly contemporary, considering all the circumstances. In some respects, it was more: it was a blueprint for the future. The editor, for example, had trusted the Dutch to do what they were only promising to do: fill in half the Zuider Zee and lay out roads and villages. His map of the Low Countries correctly anticipated that event. The same could be said of the rapidly extending grid-iron of motorways in continental Europe, the grandiose hydro-electric schemes of emergent nations . . . . and the island of Rockall, not annexed to Britain at the date of publication of the *Atlas,* but about to be, as the Bartholomew spy system had discovered.

"It's not enough," John used to tell his staff, "to be up with the times. We have to keep ahead."

The *Times Atlas,* with its hundred-odd new maps and a gazetteer in which the place-names alone added up to the length of

★ BBC Radio interview, 18th January 1960

four and a half average-sized novels, overshadowed other productions of that decade.

To complete the story of this remarkable publication, which continued beyond the death of its creator: in 1967 a 'Comprehensive' edition of the *Times Atlas* brought the principal features of the five volumes into one, added a collection of supplementary maps on world resources and threw in an illustrated guide to space flight and lunar exploration. (The first Apollo moon-landing appropriately took place two years later.)

There were four subsequent one-volume editions of the *Times Atlas* and two specially-adapted editions for those cartographical connoisseurs, the Germans.

Social and environmental changes – less space, more leisure, tighter purse-strings – were acknowledged in 1972 with a new and handsome adaptation of this large atlas in a reduced format, the *Times Concise Atlas of the World*. Up to 1976, this publication has been revised annually and supplied also in two Dutch editions. A historic offshoot, breaching the 'bamboo curtain', was the *Times Atlas of China*, published in 1974.

John Bartholomew did not live to see those modifications and adaptations and abridgments of his great five-volume work. But he lived to see the original in the bookshops, and to read the tributes paid to it.

He found time in middle age to be a member of the council of the Royal Society of Edinburgh, a trustee of the National Library of Scotland, a director of the National Bank of Scotland and an executive committee member of the National Trust for Scotland. In the tradition of the best of Scottish men of parts, he ended his life a public figure, robed in dignity. When he died in 1962 his obituarist★ doubted whether his numerous honours weighed as much with him as 'the happiness of entertaining and advising, with his ever-helpful wife, the younger generation of explorers and geographers up in Edinburgh for lectures and medal awards, in the hospitable and charming old manor house at Inveresk, whose sunny garden saw our last meeting . . . .'

The three Bartholomew sons who succeeded their father (Peter, chairman; John, cartographic director; and Robert, production director) might have kept the machine ticking over quite comfortably into the foreseeable future, following the patriarchal line, keeping it 'in the family' and ruling, as their ancestors had ruled, by unchallenged *diktat*.

Instead they decided, in 1968, to bring in new blood. They appointed a professional managing director (Mr D. A. Ross Stewart), a marketing manager (Mr M. J. Chittleburgh) and a sales supervisor (Mr Terry Egan) with a retail sales force of six to cover

★ Douglas Allan

The Board of Directors 1976
Left to Right:
M J Chittleburgh, (Marketing Director)
D A B Cunningham, (Financial Director)
D A Ross Stewart, (Managing Director)
Peter H Bartholomew, (Chairman)
Robert G Bartholomew, (Production Director)
John C Bartholomew, (Cartographic Director)

Scotland, England and Wales. For the first time in the firm's history, a Bartholomew representative called personally on booksellers, stationers and newsagents throughout Great Britain.

Over the next few years a quiet revolution in organisation and methods strengthened the marketing, costing, and production control elements. Consultation with the various departments, at different levels, is now the rule at Bartholomew's for all policy decisions and problems. The *diktat* is abolished, the 'team approach' has taken its place.

To cope with demands for more maps, and more kinds of map, Bartholomew's built a one-storey warehouse and bindery on an industrial estate at Loanhead, five miles from the Duncan Street headquarters. It enabled full use to be made of fork-lift trucks and similar handling machinery, impossible in Duncan Street because of the awkward levels.

By this time (early 1970s) the firm had established a subsidiary with Pillans & Wilson, another Edinburgh family printing business. The joint company was called B. W. Offset Limited and was to generate business for both houses – litho work for Bartholomew's and letterpress for Pillans & Wilson.

In October 1972 the Book Division was born, partly to make fuller use of the new marketing and sales departments. The emphasis is on leisure pursuits – gardening, handicrafts, collecting and the visual arts. The four years up to 1976 have been difficult ones for publishers and authors, and the Book Division has yet to produce its first best-seller.

In April 1973 Bartholomew's bought up the assets of T. & T. Clark, old and respected Edinburgh theological publishers. The Clarks had been good friends of the Bartholomews for three generations – they started coming to the firm for Bible maps in 1898 – and the new association promises to be a happy and beneficial one.

New responsibilities put space at a premium once more and in 1974 the Loanhead factory was enlarged. All these changes meant

Warehouse and Bindery, Loanhead

substantial increases in staff and Bartholomew's in 1976 employ more people than ever before – a total of 200, not including the sales force in the field and thirty-three overseas agents covering countries from Iceland to the Philippines and Chile to Hong Kong.

Through the overseas agents the firm participates in numerous Trade Fairs and Book Fairs – the biggest is the autumn Book Fair in Frankfurt, but Bartholomew maps and books are seen annually at the Sippa Exhibition in Paris, the Warsaw Book Fair, the Zagreb Spring Fair, the Jerusalem International Book Fair, the Brussels Book Fair, the World Book Fair in New Delhi and elsewhere. In 1976 Bartholomew's, on its 150th birthday, went for the first time to the Montreal Book Fair.

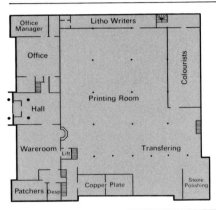

Duncan Street
Original Building in 1911

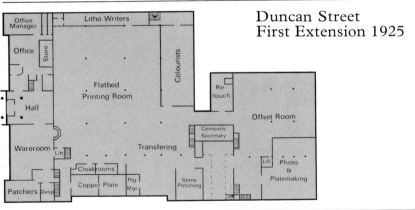

Duncan Street
First Extension 1925

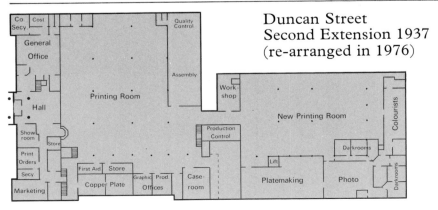

Duncan Street
Second Extension 1937
(re-arranged in 1976)

8 Looking Round & Looking Back

Walking long ago at five o'clock in the morning down Park Road, in an era when some old residents still called it Gibbet Loan, you might hear half a dozen voices trolling a shanty in the Bartholomew basement. The chorus was led by an ex-seafaring man, Davie Crole. The men were rhythmically swinging the flywheel of the gas engine which powered the printing machinery.

Continuity of service at the top is usually reflected at all levels in a family firm. The roll-call of long-serving employees is often

This historic photograph was taken in 1960 to mark the presentation to Mr Allan Dick for 50 years service in the firm.
Standing left to right:
James Lewis, Chief Cartographer
Nan Tear, Colourist
James Park MBE, Office Manager
Robert Trotter, Foreman Printer
Alexander Williamson, Senior Draughtsman
William Dickson MBE, Production Manager
John Bennett, Mounting Room Manager.
Sitting left to right:
George Paterson, Foreman Printer
David Webster, Copper Plate Printer
Dr John Bartholomew CBE, Chairman
Allan Dick, Packer (formerly Printer)
John Davies, Foreman Engraver
Elizabeth Cameron, Editorial Staff

one which many a much larger company would be proud of.★
When those of recent vintage foregather, or pay a nostalgic call in
Duncan Street, one sees the Bartholomew milestones reaching
back, and 1826 seems not so long ago after all. To them, some
departments are new and some are old – but all represent the
organic growth of a healthy and tightly-knit organisation, and the
changes in them mark logical steps in the progress and prosperity
of John Bartholomew & Son Limited.

★ See list of long-serving employees, Appendix II

George Paterson and Alan Dick, printers preparing for retirement around 1960, clearly remembered the old flywheel. They remembered also the rat hunts in the old Parkside Works (the rats lived in the railway rubbish tip next door, and ran along the steam pipes). The printers could tell tales of Edward Stanton, paper storeman and lamplighter and custodian of the gas mantels which illuminated the works. They remembered their own apprenticeships and the old-time printers and transferrers (who transferred the image to stone for lithographic work) . . . . they still spoke with awe of the seniors of their day – Charlie Loch's is a name all the veterans remember – who could tell, in their turn, anecdotes of John junior and John senior and the dawn of Bartholomew history.

The advance of technology and the evolution of the departments out of the past and into the present have brought changes which will continue as long as science finds new ways of improving map-making techniques. The following descriptions of departments are necessarily brief:

Patching department. The patcher's job was to arrange type and art work on and around a plate before it was reproduced. He added the borders, inserted the scale of the map and found space for the explanatory notes. As a department, patching went back to the 1890s; but it was something of an anachronism in an expanding business, for it was staffed by one or two men at the most and the only reason it remained so long a separate department was that neither printing nor artists' unions would recognise the occupation. John Colquhoun, last of the patchers, was the only non-union employee at Bartholomew's, apart from the colourists and the office staff. Out of the patchers of yesteryear there has evolved the editorial department of today.

Editorial department. The team of ten cartographic editors has been built up to prepare detailed design specifications for new products and to keep existing maps up to date. The editors sift through the mass of reference material which streams in continually to them and insert their revision instructions on the 'correction copies' of maps and gazetteers. The correction of maps used to be the task of the drawing office; its members would supply marked copies for the 'writers' (latterly the photo draughtsmen), who then applied the corrections to glass plate or film. But now the draughtsmen have lost the job of correcting – not without regret, for it introduced a little variety into their day – and they have to concentrate on the more specialised skills of their trade.

Photo department. The department dates from 1925. A Hunter Penrose camera took shots of the copper plate impressions and specially-trained colourists painted in the shapes for the different colours, the shading being varied by mechanical screening and stippling processes. As time went by, all the stone colourists of the old 'tint stones' department graduated into photo colourists. The last chieftainess of 'tint stones' was Miss Nan Tear, who

The Drawing Office

Right: New process camera – Klimsch Super Autohorika 101K 40 x 42 ins. Inset, Old process camera – Hunter Penrose Gallery Camera 30 x 40 ins.

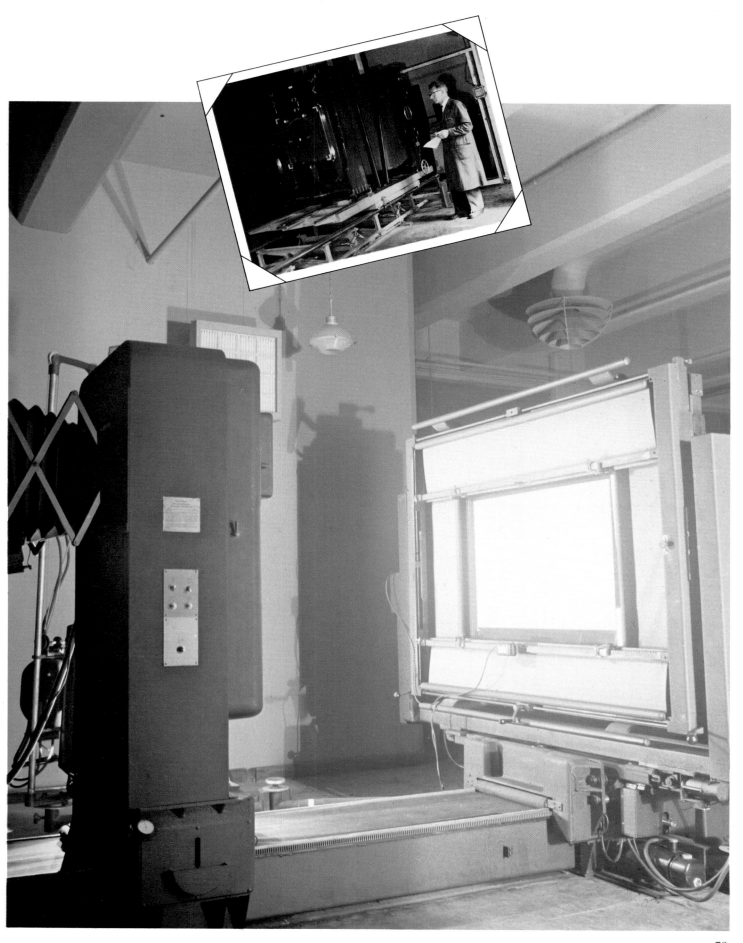

retired in 1963 after more than fifty years with the firm.

Until about 1950 the photo department used glass plates which were sensitised with silver nitrate and immersed in a preservative of liquid coffee. Pre-sensitised plates replaced them and Bartholomew's had experimented successfully enough by 1965 to be able to dispense altogether with their heavy and bulky outfit of plates.

The names chiefly associated with this department's history are those of George Kerr, who headed it from 1927, and his son Clifford Kerr, who was a technical director in the firm at the time of his retirement in 1970. In their time they presided over the introduction of bigger and more elaborate cameras and darkroom equipment, which culminated in the arrival of the versatile Klimsch (42″ x 45″) in 1962. Under John Leisnham, its current head, a further expansion of the photo department is being planned in 1976.

Platemaking department. Platemaking came in with photography and the two departments evolved together. Originally zinc plates were used. To produce sixteen pages of an atlas you set up four quarters of four pages in a printing frame and exposed them one at a time in contact with the printing plate. It was a procedure which demanded a high degree of concentration from the person who lined up the pages with the register marks. After 1930 a series of step-and-repeat machines minimised the effects of human error and the zinc plates yielded to plates of anodised aluminium. Those in use in 1976 are mostly made of pre-sensitised aluminium and bimetal.

The change from glass photo plates to film had saved space; the Protocol Register system introduced in 1971 saved time. With this system a pile of film sheets can be lined up, pinned down and held firm with mathematical exactitude.

Traditionally the platemaking department at Bartholomew's is responsible for 'proofs' – the check copies of work in hand, on which any faults or imperfections are discovered and rectified before the machine starts its run of impressions.

Printing department. When the firm moved to Duncan Street before the first World War, John George Bartholomew set out fourteen flat-bed lithographic machines in the new printing room. The room was a model of its kind, with overhead windows and the exciting novelty of electric arc-lighting. The machines were each driven by an electric motor, of which the control panel (a member of the family recalls) 'gleamed with brass switches mounted on marble.'

The first off-set rotary printing machines arrived in 1925, when the Duncan Street premises were first extended. Those responsible for them found they were expected to be mechanics as well as printers. Willie Dickson bore the brunt of a frustrating running-in period. He survived it, and finished his career as production director. It was also at that period that the photo department came into being, to provide photo-printed plates for the rotary presses.

Piece by piece, Bartholomew's added to their machinery collection. By the 1960s they had something of a museum of printing history, for one of the Victorian flat-beds was retained and upstairs the lithographer pursued his art and samples from the whole range of techniques ancient and modern were in use, down to the most up-to-date off-sets, costing £50,000 apiece. Another extension had had to be built in 1938 to accommodate the two-colour Crabtree presses (quad demy), which were especially suited to the production of school and reference atlases.

Up to the beginning of World War Two, one expected to pay about £3000 for a new printing machine. The four-colour Roland press which Bartholomew's installed in the 1960s – they were the first firm in the United Kingdom to order one – cost about £50,000. The Roland 800 which the firm invested in ten years later was a staggering £136,879 – yet not quite as staggering as it sounds, since it had about eighty times the output of an old flat-bed. This is why Bartholomew's have managed to keep their printing costs relatively steady throughout the years.

The latest four colour off-set press – Roland 804-5

In Edwardian days, the annual total of impressions turned out by the firm amounted to seven millions. In 1975 the figure was well over a hundred millions, an output for which three four-colour and two two-colour presses were responsible.

The Bindery. At Bartholomew's this department was always called the Mounting Room. It took care of mounting, trimming and folding – all the end-processes of map and atlas-making. For many years the firm mounted its maps by hand and the big mounting room was redolent of the paste and water mixture which was stirred in large tubs. (Present-day Bartholomews say that the family has a hereditary aversion to cornflour on that account.) You pasted up your map on the flat table, laid your square of cloth or jaconnet on it, pasted another map on top . . . . and so on until they formed a tall soggy pile, which then had to be left to settle and partially dry out. Each map with its backing was then detached and hung up on one of the ropes which stretched from side to side of the room, until the whole place was festooned in maps.

When they were dry, you reconstituted your pile, this time 'in register' – that is, with all the sides and corners matching, ready for trimming with the guillotine.

Dissected maps underwent a further process, which meant that they cost a few pence more to the customer. Having been drawn, hung and – so to speak – quartered (cut into sections of the map's folded size) they were pasted straight on to an unrolled bolt of cloth pinned along the wall. Bartholomew's used no mechanical aid for this job; its neatness depended on the experienced eye and touch of the mounter.

Folding Machines at Loanhead

Dissected maps are today a thing of the past, which distresses some map-lovers. But economic factors over the past quarter-century have made it increasingly difficult to maintain the range, as the statistics for the famous Half-inch series show. The Half-inch in paper, in 1950, sold 100,000, twelve years later 215,000, twelve years after that 349,000. The Half-inch in cloth, in the same years, sold 200,000, then 158,000 and then dropped to 46,000 in 1974 (not a complete year: they were already being withdrawn). The dissected Half-inch sold 6,250 in 1950, but only 1,500 in 1963. In 1974 they were withdrawn.

When the Half-inch series comes to the end of its record-breaking run of a hundred years and is superseded by the new National series (metric, 1 : 100,000), neither dissected nor cloth maps will be available, except for special orders at a price deliberately designed to discourage buyers.

People who complained that once they got a map opened up they could never get it shut again might have taken lessons from the girls at Bartholomew's, who used to fold maps at high speed with the dexterity of a sharper riffling his own pack of cards. Up to twenty years ago, all Bartholomew folding maps were folded by hand – a task as tedious and long-drawn-out as any the apprentices of James Bain's day must have known, since it was not unusual for 50,000 copies to be required. Different sizes of maps required different folding procedures and it was not until 1970 that satisfactory machinery was devised to take the laborious operation of map-folding out of the hands of the girls.

The Stahl folding machines, which are capable of undertaking complex folding patterns – continuous, square, parallel, right angle, concertina and staggered concertina and all sorts of combinations of those designs, are now in operation at the Loanhead factory. Besides meeting all their own folding requirements, Bartholomew's provide a folding service for other printers and publishers.

Royal Visit – 30th June 1971 HRH The Duke of Edinburgh and HRH The Princess Anne with the Chairman and Marketing Director

9 In 1976

The building has a noble façade – columns, capital and pediment – but it needs a vista. It faces the narrow street and you come sidelong to its proportions, as to some Athenian temple reconstructed in an overgrown suburb of the Piraeus. It would have been more of a landmark a century and a half ago, with only the university dome and the Royal Infirmary tower across the Meadows to out-top it – one temple of healing and two of learning, dominating the south Edinburgh skyline.

You make out the blackened legend on the entablature, EDINBURGH GEOGRAPHICAL INSTITUTE, and reflect on the awe which that title must have aroused when new, such as the words SPACE LABORATORY might arouse in more recent times. Geography, when that inscription was chiselled, had an aura of the occult about it, an esoteric mystery which Bartholomew's helped to dispel.

You step inside, on to a tessellated floor whose cracks are a memento of the heavy burden of paper stocks which it bore when the *Times Atlas* of 1922 was preparing. A great globe confronts you, hanging in chains. It was displayed on the Bartholomew stand at the Wembley Exhibition of 1924. It is housed in a classical rotunda and above it runs a fragment of Ciceronian dialogue, roughly to be translated:

'How fortunate is he who, engaged in trivial affairs, can keep in mind the vastness of the whole world.'

Turn right or left and you are dazzled by the cartographical fashion parade, the maps in their new-season jackets. Some, it must be admitted, would cause Dr John George Bartholomew to raise an eyebrow. This Football History map, for example, with insets of the coloured jerseys and crests of the clubs . . . . this Children's Map of London, complete with nursery rhymes . . . . this Clan Map, 'Scotland of Old', with all the armorial bearings of the clan chiefs and warnings of dire penalties for those who improperly appropriate them. This is carrying 'special maps' into dimensions John George could scarcely have apprehended.

The map-making business of 1976, however, is a globe with many facets. Along with serious scholarship and scientific research goes the perfectly laudable aim of interesting people and entertaining them and catering for various interests.

Here is a splendid, glossy, inexpensive publication: 'What to See Where' – a map of Scotland for first-time sightseers, foreign tourists particularly, showing the well-known and not-so-well-known curiosities of the land, from Norse grave-chambers in Orkney to the Jim Clark (racing motorist) Memorial Room at Duns in the Border country.

Here are Bonnie Prince Charlie's Wanderings, reproduced from the drawings of Colonel Grante and superimposed on an up-to-date map – a good example of the nudge towards education and enlightenment which has been Bartholomew policy through the ages. It is a weekend touring project you might never have thought of: tracing the routes of the Young Chevalier through the

The Rotunda and Entrance Hall, Duncan Street

western Highlands. The map puts the idea into your head and simultaneously offers you the means of accomplishing it.

The Business Planning Map of Great Britain, published in association with *The Times* newspaper, concentrates on airports, freight-liner terminals and depots, motorways and rail links and the areas covered by television transmitters. It is designed to help the businessman move his merchandise and communicate with his customers. This map is supplied in hanging strips, or rolled up in a tube, or mounted on a board and framed . . . . whichever you desire. And there are spaces left in the information columns, so that you can add the memoranda relevant to your own business.

Running an eye quickly over the display board, you note a *Mini Pocket Atlas,* a *Road Atlas Europe,* a Glasgow Area Wall Map and several 'To and Through' maps of different cities, for the benefit of visiting motorists . . . . the well-known series of GT motoring maps with the chequered flag on them . . . . anglers' maps, antiquities maps, battlefield maps, historic buildings maps, castle maps and civic coats-of-arms maps, the positions of the Armada wrecks, the military roads and garrisons of Scotland. How many Britons planning a holiday know that there are Bartholomew maps on sale which indicate all the sandy beaches?

The Blaeu maps catch the eye. Blaeu did the early maps of Scotland, county by county, with picturesque titles like Braid-Allaban & Athole, Lothian & Linlitquo, Extima Scotiae. Bartholomew's brought them out again a few years ago and copied them so authentically, on antique paper, that two German publishers wanted to buy them with the trade-mark deleted, in order to pass them off as originals.

The royal coat-of-arms and 'Cartographer by Appointment' which used to decorate the blue cover of the Half-inch is not much in evidence. The appointment lapsed with John Bartholomew's death in 1962 and was not restored until 1974. What misdemeanour was the firm guilty of? "None," says the chairman. "It lapsed automatically on the death of the grantee. I could have applied at once for it to be renewed. But we were a new team, and managerial changes were in the air. We decided that the Royal Warrant was something we ought to make ourselves worthy of before we accepted it again."

The superficial change of recent years has been in the style and presentation of the atlases. Queen of large concise atlases, the *Times* (which has gone into several foreign editions, all of which have a content and arrangement suited to the nation they are produced for) wears a smart, beautifully-printed jacket which combines restraint with modernity and will not look out of place on the most contemporary coffee-table. So does the *Times Atlas of the Moon:* that satellite has been a challenge to cartographers as well as astronauts.

In point of numbers produced and distributed, the *Reader's Digest Atlas* is far ahead of the field these days. Bartholomew's do most of the maps for this big popular collection, which also has its

150th Anniversary Celebration Luncheon 4th June 1976
Leslie Gardiner, Author of the History, **Professor Ronald Miller,** Principal Guest and President of the Royal Scottish Geographical Society with the Company Chairman

85

specially made-up and foreign-language editions for sixteen countries. The total in 1976 is seven and a half million copies.

All the new publications proclaim an extraordinary advance in format and design on the ocean liners, Britannias with trident and the rising suns of sixty years ago.

In the drawing office they are doing a relief map of Spain. Unexpectedly, a great deal still depends on the patience, the practised hand and judicious eye of the draughtsman. Turn this map upside down and the shading on the slopes of the mountains looks all wrong. Turn it the right way up and you have a graphic impression of the harsh grandeur of the sierra. It is like a conjuring trick, yet the draughtsman appears to be pencilling it in haphazardly. How does he do it?

"You use your imagination," he says. "You start off by imagining the light is coming from the north-west. It's the only way to convey a true impression. Don't ask me why."

Someone else is revising the last of the celebrated Half-inch, a map which the motorist and walker of today have learned to value as highly as did the horseback and penny-farthing rider of ninety years ago. The editor is removing a small patch of emerald green and substituting a small patch of blue – hours of patient toil, and all because a water board has decided to increase the capacity of a Welsh reservoir. To cover all the implications of such a change, it is necessary to consult many sources. In this case, probably, the Youth Hostels Association, the Nature Conservancy Board, the Men of the Trees, the Rights of Way societies, the National Trust and the Wildlife Trust and the Countryside Commission were only the start of it. At some stage a dyeline print may have to go to the Welsh Language Society to see if there are any objections to the spelling.

In what is still known as the mounting room, editors are correcting sheets of maps, tiny square by tiny square, and consulting their files of notes. The notes are a record of the despatches from innumerable agencies which notify topographical changes all over the world. The Post Office has announced a couple of minor amendments to boundary lines on the new Postal Code map of Somerset. From the Center for Short-Lived Phenomena at Cambridge, Massachusetts, notification cards are flocking in by every mail, for it is the time of the Turkish earthquake. This naturally means alterations on the World Map of Earthquakes which Bartholomew's produce. The conventional sign for an earthquake must be inserted in a new area of Anatolia and that sign will be changed to a date – 1975 – as soon as the death-toll reaches one thousand.

Submarine earthquakes, eruptions and disturbances sometimes involve major changes – as in Iceland, in recent times, where whole new islands have been thrown up and in some cases have subsided again.

In a corner of this room sits Miss Gray, young in looks but senior in service, and reads the newspaper while others work. But she is working too. Her job is to study every line of *The Times* every day and to make out an index card and reference for any news item which may affect cartography, either in the near future or twenty years from now.

Here in the mounting room you can make out the marks of the old hooks and rails from which the map-hanging ropes used to be stretched. Upstairs, in what is now being arranged as a map library, you find the panelling pitted with tack marks: those long walls used to support the roll of cloth on which dissected sections of maps were pinned, when it was all done by hand.

In the printing room you can identify, from lines in the concrete flooring, the shapes of the old machines which were brought over from Park Road in 1911. A flat, thick lithographic stone is lying somewhere about, and one of the trolleys on to which six men lifted it. But much of the space down here is bought up with the huge and intricate bulk of the Roland presses and the paper stocks and the wind-tunnel through which the paper is passed to be conditioned when it arrives from the papermaker.

The Klimsch camera is like the cameras we knew as children, but tremendously enlarged, with a concertina hood which might have come out of a horror movie. The darkroom behind this monstrosity is probably slightly larger than the attic room in which John Bartholomew senior first 'reduced Persia' and 'finished off North Germany.'

Finally, a visit to David Webster in the small back room. He stands over a burnished copper plate with a magnifying glass to his eye. In 1976 there is only one copper-plate map engraver (we might have guessed he worked for Bartholomew's) and this is he. The craft he follows is much the same as that which John senior learned to follow – a craft which, when John senior was born in the year of Trafalgar, had been in existence without major change for at least three centuries.

The house of Bartholomew was founded on fine copper engraving, and the copper-plate engraver was the key figure in its history until modern times. By his touch the reputation of a business was made or marred. Like a surgeon, he had his tray of delicate instruments and, like a surgeon performing a brain operation, he performed his delicate task.

Mr Webster cannot say how old these instruments, sixty or seventy of them, may be. They were handed down to him. Perhaps they antedate Bartholomew's itself although, like the Irishman's pocket-knife, they will have had their three new blades and two new handles in their time. They are shaped and sharpened by their owner (but who will he hand them down to?) and they closely resemble the 'gravers' which the first of the Bartholomews used; which themselves resembled those tools wielded by the anonymous craftsman who cut the first World Projection of Gerhard Mercator in the 1500s.

The burin, with its lozenge-shaped head, takes its name from the 'burr' (a roughened ridge) which it makes along the edge of the line it is engraving. The next tool is for hairlines, the next for curves, the next for cutting thin parallel lines. Here is the dotter, which makes dots; here the town stamp, which puts in the circular symbol, inked or blank, to denote centres of population; here the roulette, a serrated wheel for running pecked lines; here the line gauge for making faint erasable scratches to keep the lettering straight.

You cannot buy them in the hardware shop. David Webster's line gauge is made of a watchspring and a knitting needle. His point, or stylus, has for the past thirty years been a common steel

Engraver's equipment photographed on a copper plate.
Left to right: (top) 3 gauges, curve, parallel rule. (bottom) 3 ring punches, magnifying glass, burnisher, peck roulette, round graver, flat graver, dot roulette lozenge graver, wide dot roulette, scraper

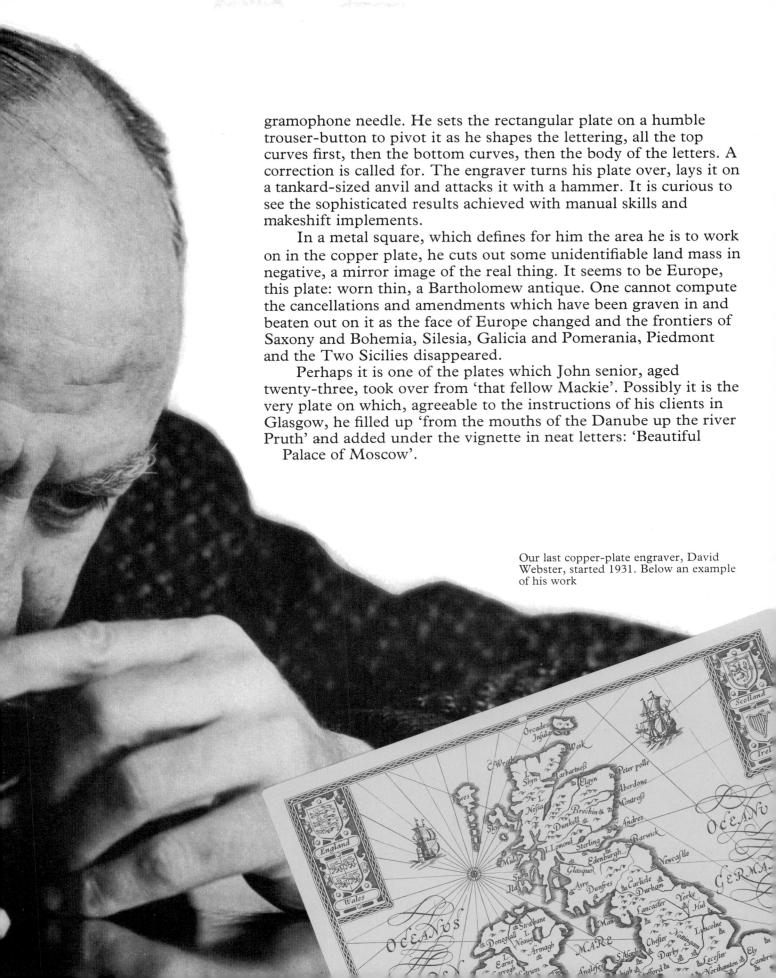

gramophone needle. He sets the rectangular plate on a humble trouser-button to pivot it as he shapes the lettering, all the top curves first, then the bottom curves, then the body of the letters. A correction is called for. The engraver turns his plate over, lays it on a tankard-sized anvil and attacks it with a hammer. It is curious to see the sophisticated results achieved with manual skills and makeshift implements.

In a metal square, which defines for him the area he is to work on in the copper plate, he cuts out some unidentifiable land mass in negative, a mirror image of the real thing. It seems to be Europe, this plate: worn thin, a Bartholomew antique. One cannot compute the cancellations and amendments which have been graven in and beaten out on it as the face of Europe changed and the frontiers of Saxony and Bohemia, Silesia, Galicia and Pomerania, Piedmont and the Two Sicilies disappeared.

Perhaps it is one of the plates which John senior, aged twenty-three, took over from 'that fellow Mackie'. Possibly it is the very plate on which, agreeable to the instructions of his clients in Glasgow, he filled up 'from the mouths of the Danube up the river Pruth' and added under the vignette in neat letters: 'Beautiful Palace of Moscow'.

Our last copper-plate engraver, David Webster, started 1931. Below an example of his work

Letter from Sir John Murray

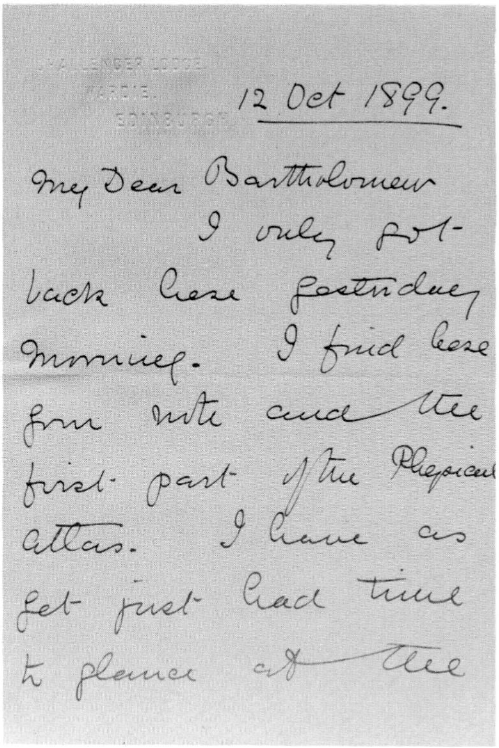

CHALLENGER LODGE
WARDIE
EDINBURGH

12 Oct 1899.

My Dear Bartholomew
I only got
back here yesterday
morning. I find here
your note and the
first part of the Physical
Atlas. I have as
yet just had time
to glance at the

Letter from Prof. J. Geikie

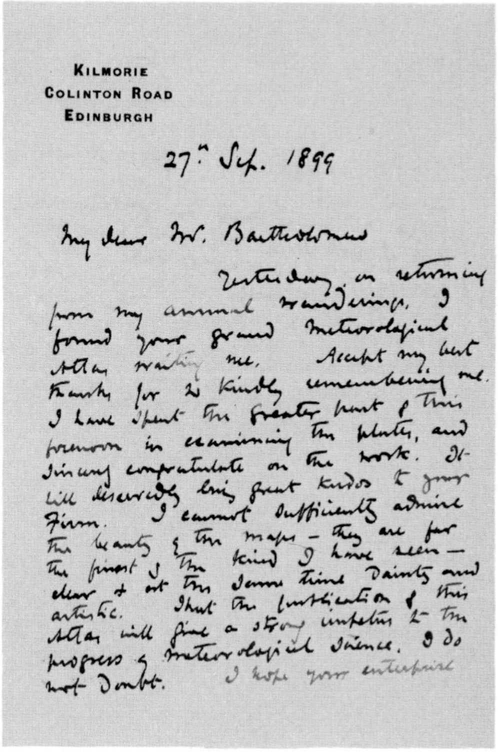

KILMORIE
COLINTON ROAD
EDINBURGH

27ᵗʰ Sep. 1899

My dear Mr. Bartholomew
Yesterday, on returning
from my annual wanderings, I
found your grand Meteorological
Atlas waiting me. Accept my best
thanks for so kindly remembering me.
I have spent the greater part of this
forenoon in examining the plates, and
in any congratulate on the work. It
will deservedly bring great kudos to your
Firm. I cannot sufficiently admire
the beauty of the maps — they are far
the finest of the kind I have seen —
clear & at the same time dainty and
artistic. That the publication of this
Atlas will give a strong impetus to the
progress of Meteorological Science I do
not doubt. I hope your enterprise

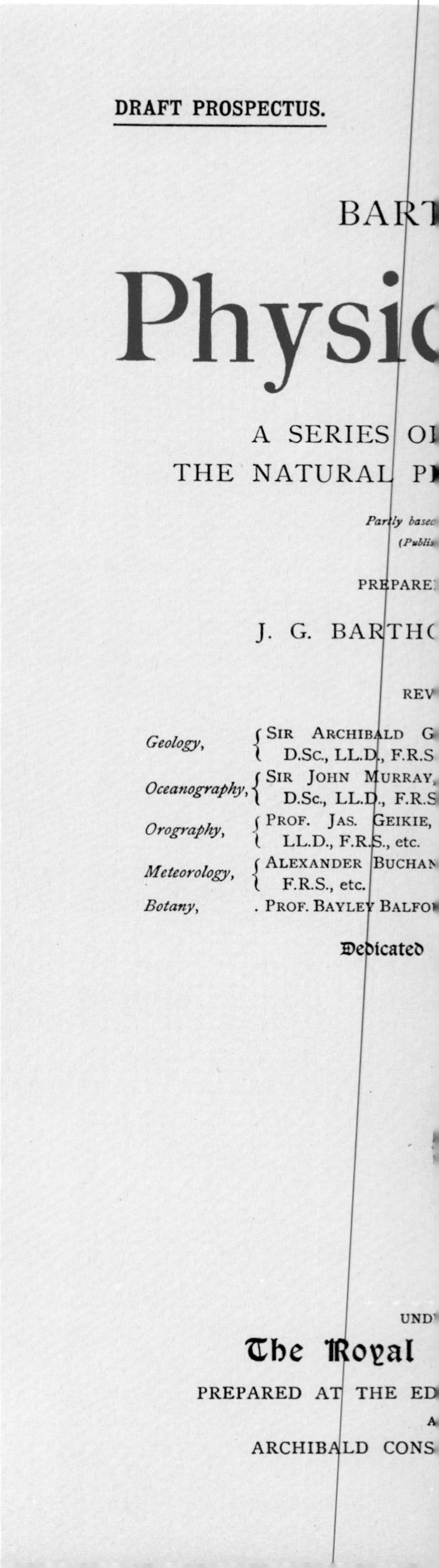

DRAFT PROSPECTUS.

BART

Physic

A SERIES OF
THE NATURAL P

Partly based
(Publis

PREPARE

J. G. BARTHO

REV

Geology, { SIR ARCHIBALD G
{ D.Sc, LL.D., F.R.S
Oceanography, { SIR JOHN MURRAY
{ D.Sc, LL.D., F.R.S
Orography, { PROF. JAS. GEIKIE,
{ LL.D., F.R.S., etc.
Meteorology, { ALEXANDER BUCHAN
{ F.R.S., etc.
Botany, . PROF. BAYLEY BALFOU

Dedicated

UND

The Royal

PREPARED AT THE ED
A
ARCHIBALD CONS

MEW'S

Atlas

LLUSTRATING

A OF THE EARTH

alischer Atlas"
ha, 1889-92)

IRECTION OF

F.R.S.E., F.R.G.S.

ED BY

ogy, { P. L. SCLATER, D.SC., LL.D.,
{ F.Z.S.

ography, PROF. A. H. KEANE, F.R.G.S.

ography, PROF. ELISÉE RECLUS.

nography, { PROF. RALPH COPELAND,
{ F.R.A.S., Astronomer-
{ Royal for Scotland.

rnetism, { PROF. C. G. KNOTT, D.SC.,
{ F.R.S.E.

o the Queen

GE OF

hical Society

OGRAPHICAL INSTITUTE

BY

CO., WESTMINSTER

Letter from the Personal Secretary to
Queen Victoria

November 3
1898

BALMORAL CASTLE.

Sir

In Sir Arthur
Bigge's absence I
am commanded by
the Queen to thank
you for the first
volume of your
very interesting Physical

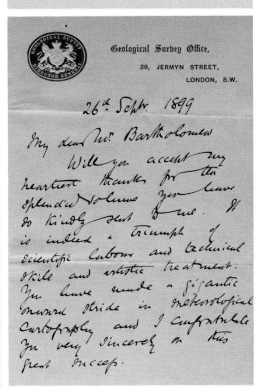

Letter from Sir Archibald Geikie

Geological Survey Office,
28, JERMYN STREET,
LONDON, S.W.

26th Septr. 1899

My dear Mr. Bartholomew
Will you accept my
heartiest thanks for the
splendid volume you have
so kindly sent to me. It
is indeed a triumph of
scientific labour and technical
skill and artistic treatment.
You have made a gigantic
onward stride in meteorological
cartography and I congratulate
you very sincerely on this
great success.

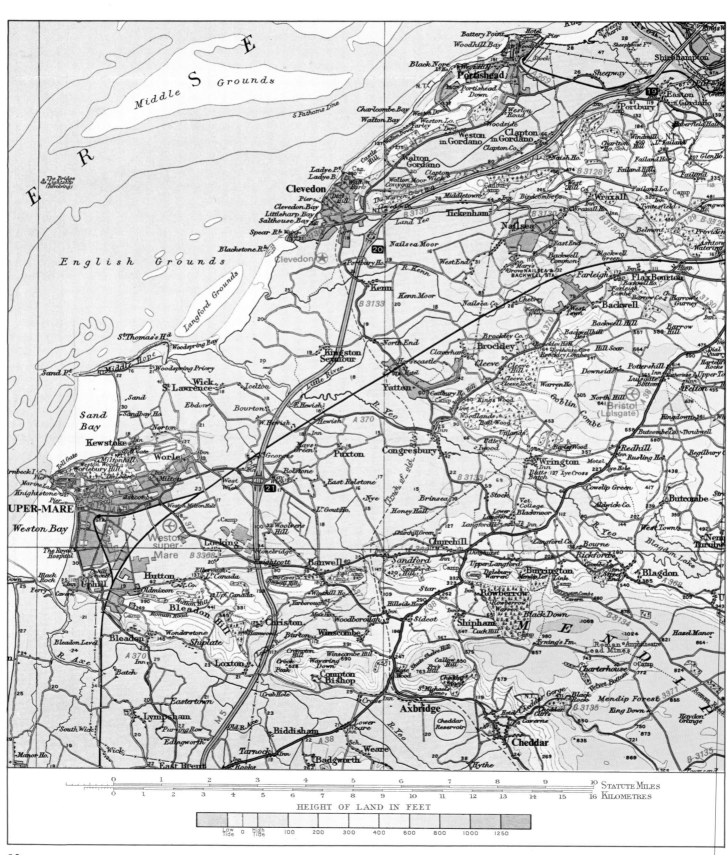

STATUTE MILES

KILOMETRES

HEIGHT OF LAND IN FEET

Low tide 0 High Tide 100 200 300 400 600 800 1000 1250

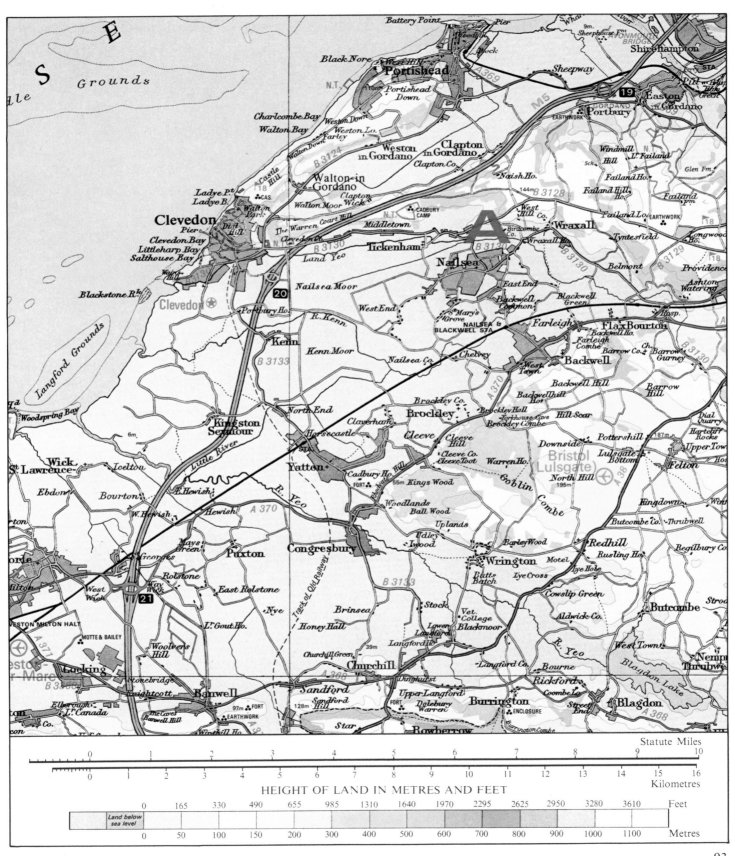

HEIGHT OF LAND IN METRES AND FEET

		0	165	330	490	655	985	1310	1640	1970	2295	2625	2950	3280	3610	Feet
	Land below sea level															
		0	50	100	150	200	300	400	500	600	700	800	900	1000	1100	Metres

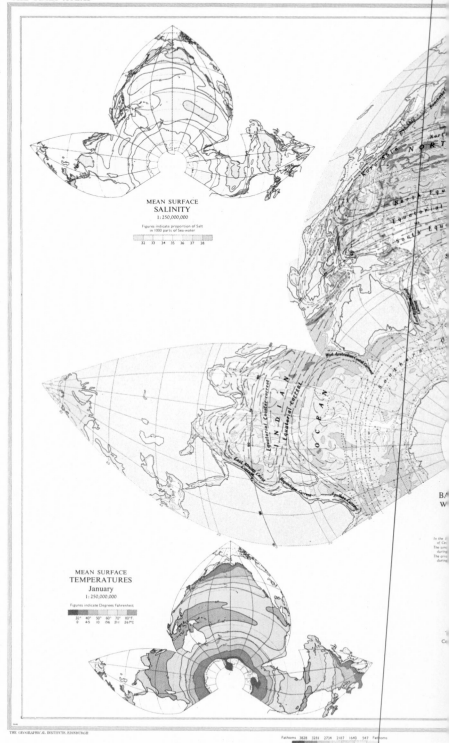

MEAN SURFACE
SALINITY
1:250,000,000

Figures indicate proportion of Salt
in 1000 parts of Sea-water

32 33 34 35 36 37 38

MEAN SURFACE
TEMPERATURES
January
1:250,000,000

Figures indicate Degrees Fahrenheit

32° 40° 50° 60° 70° 80°F.
0   4·5 10 15·6 21·1 26·7°C

THE GEOGRAPHICAL INSTITUTE, EDINBURGH

Fathoms 3828 3281 2734 2187 1640 547 Fathoms
Metres 7000 6000 5000 4000 3000 1000 Metres

'World Oceanography' spread from the
Times Atlas showing the Lotus projection

94

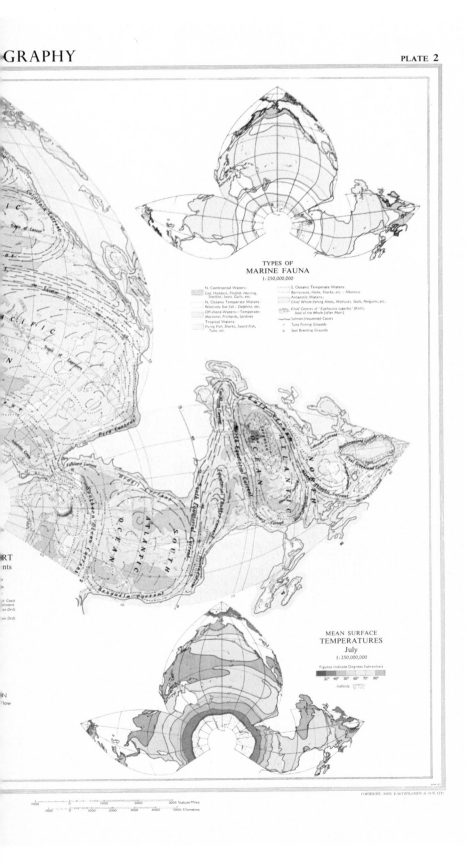

TYPES OF
MARINE FAUNA
1 : 250,000,000

N. Continental Waters:
  Cod, Haddock, Flatfish, Herring,
  Shellfish, Seals, Gulls, etc.
N. Oceanic Temperate Waters:
  Relatively few fish : Dolphins, etc.
Off-shore Waters—Temperate:
  Mackerel, Pilchards, Sardines
Tropical Waters:
  Flying Fish, Sharks, Sword Fish,
  Tuna, etc.

S. Oceanic Temperate Waters:
  Barracouta, Hake, Sharks, etc. : Albatross
Antarctic Waters:
  Chief Whale-fishing Areas, Walruses, Seals, Penguins, etc.
Chief Centres of 'Euthausia superba' (Krill),
  food of the Whale (after Marr)
Salmon-frequented Coasts
  Tuna Fishing Grounds
  Seal Breeding Grounds

MEAN SURFACE
TEMPERATURES
July
1 : 250,000,000

Figures indicate Degrees Fahrenheit

32° 40° 50° 60° 70° 80°

Icefields

1000 0 1000 2000 3000 Statute Miles
1000 0 1000 2000 3000 4000 5000 Kilometres

Clan Map of Scotland

Scenic Map of Scotland

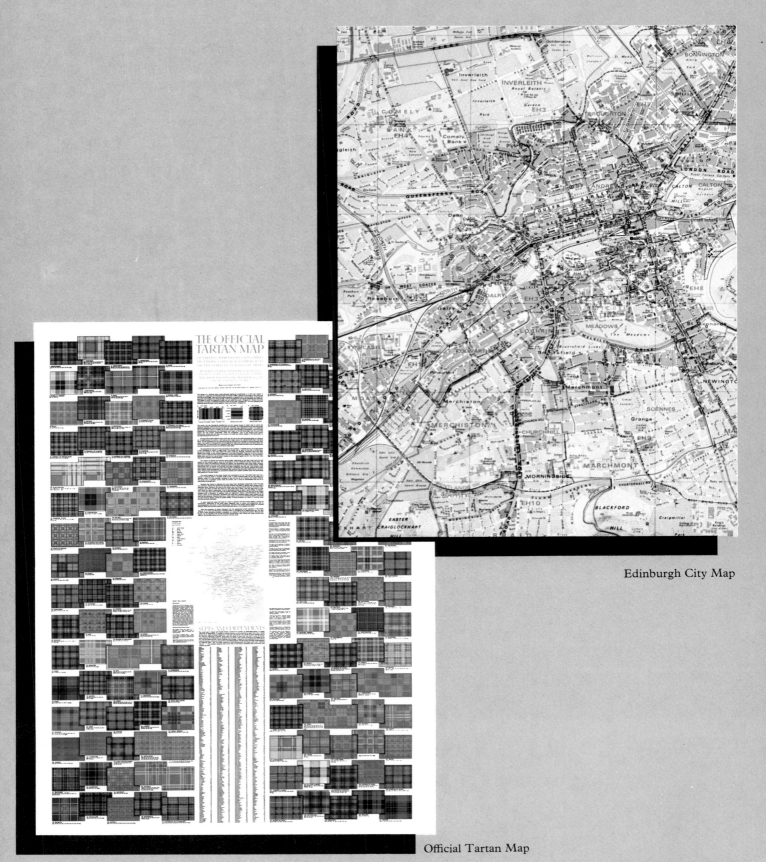

Edinburgh City Map

Official Tartan Map

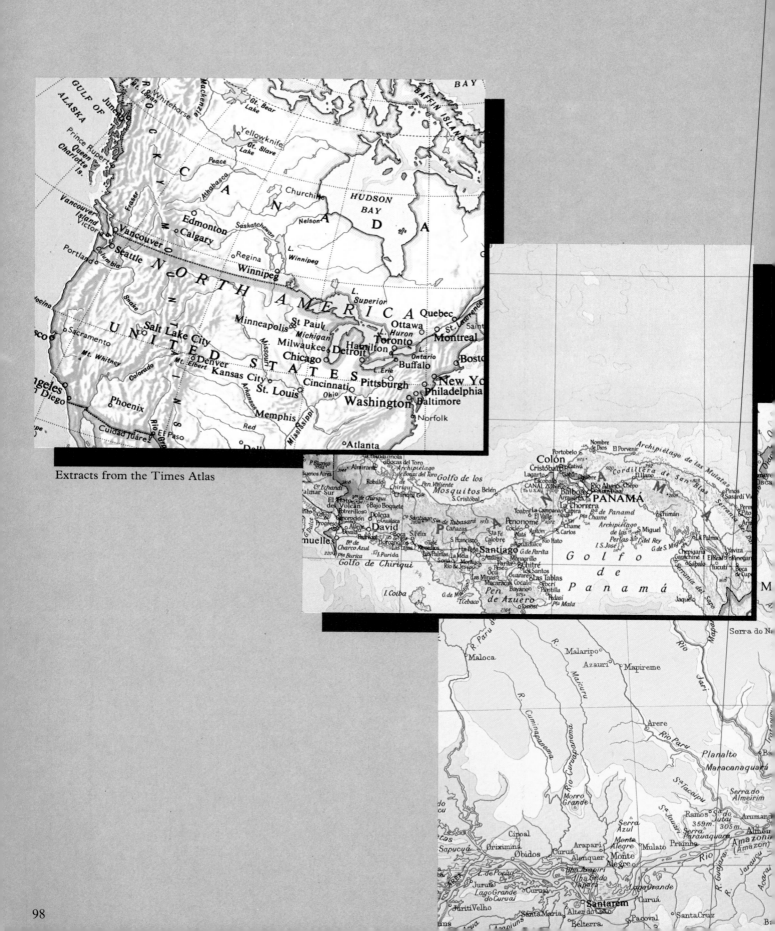

Extracts from the Times Atlas

98

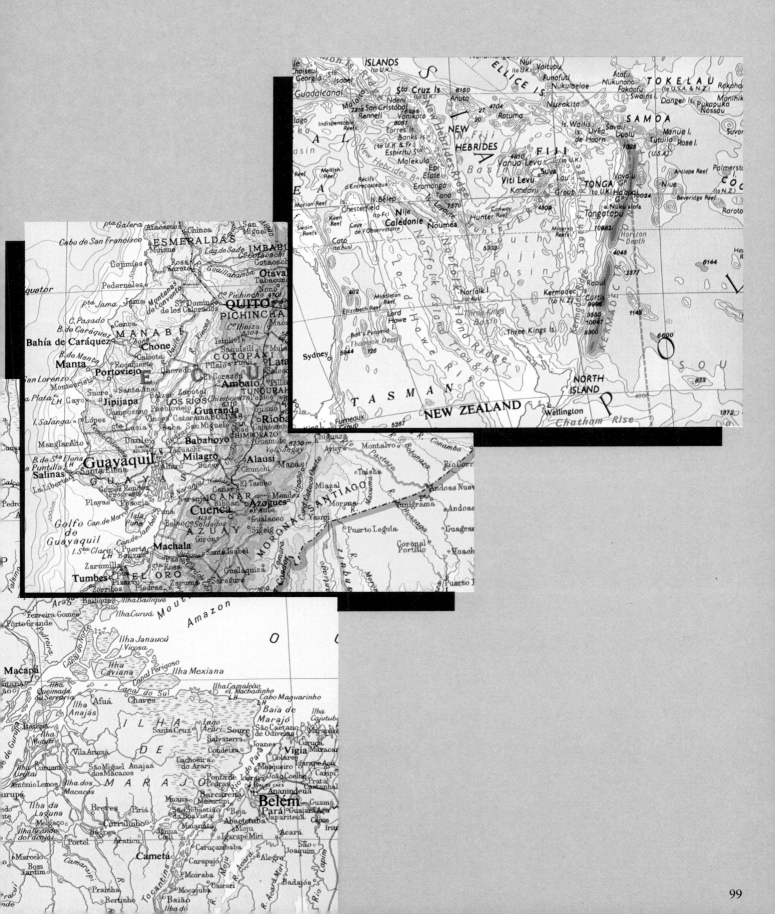

99

WORLD NATURAL DISASTE

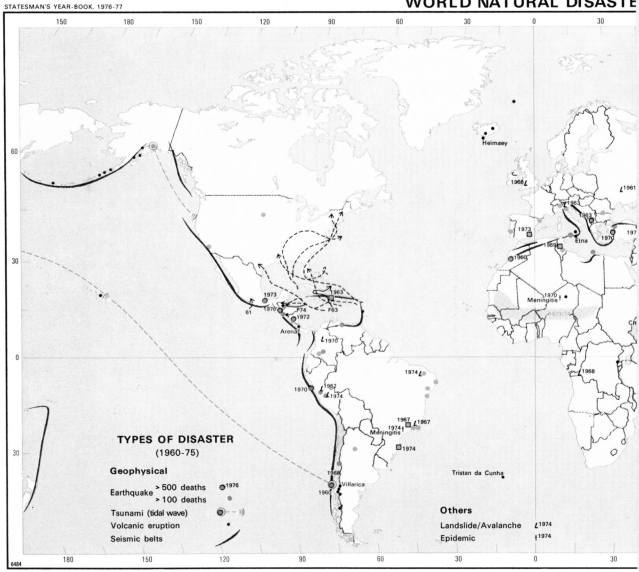

TYPES OF DISASTER
(1960-75)

Geophysical

Earthquake > 500 deaths   ● 1976
> 100 deaths   ●

Tsunami (tidal wave)   ◎ — ⟩⟩⟩

Volcanic eruption   ●

Seismic belts

Others

Landslide/Avalanche   ∠ 1974

Epidemic   † 1974

Heimaey

Etna

Meningitis

Arenal

Villarica

Tristan da Cunha

6484

1:110 000 000

World Natural Disasters Map from the
Statesman's Year Book

Regional Development in the EEC Map
from the Statesman's Year Book

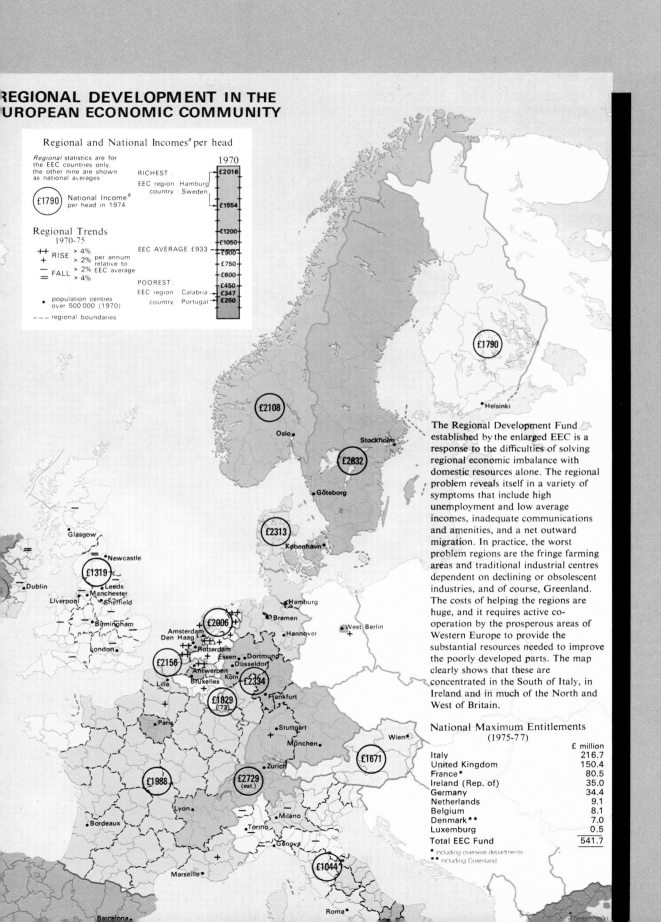

REGIONAL DEVELOPMENT IN THE EUROPEAN ECONOMIC COMMUNITY

Regional and National Incomes[a] per head

Regional statistics are for the EEC countries only. the other nine are shown as national averages

£1790 — National Income[a] per head in 1974

Regional Trends 1970-75

++ RISE > 4%
+ > 2% per annum relative to
─ > 2% EEC average
≡ FALL > 4%

• population centres over 500 000 (1970)

- - - regional boundaries

1970

RICHEST :
EEC region : Hamburg
country : Sweden

£2016
£1554
£1200
£1050
£900
EEC AVERAGE £933
£750
£600
£450
£347
£250

POOREST :
EEC region : Calabria
country : Portugal

The Regional Development Fund established by the enlarged EEC is a response to the difficulties of solving regional economic imbalance with domestic resources alone. The regional problem reveals itself in a variety of symptoms that include high unemployment and low average incomes, inadequate communications and amenities, and a net outward migration. In practice, the worst problem regions are the fringe farming areas and traditional industrial centres dependent on declining or obsolescent industries, and of course, Greenland. The costs of helping the regions are huge, and it requires active co-operation by the prosperous areas of Western Europe to provide the substantial resources needed to improve the poorly developed parts. The map clearly shows that these are concentrated in the South of Italy, in Ireland and in much of the North and West of Britain.

National Maximum Entitlements (1975-77)

	£ million
Italy	216.7
United Kingdom	150.4
France*	80.5
Ireland (Rep. of)	35.0
Germany	34.4
Netherlands	9.1
Belgium	8.1
Denmark**	7.0
Luxemburg	0.5
Total EEC Fund	541.7

* including overseas departments
** including Greenland

J. BARTHOLOMEW'S GEOGRAPHICAL ESTABLISHMENT

MAPS & ATLASES

EDUCATIONAL MAPS

TOURIST'S MAPS

MAPS FOR GUIDE BOOKS

RAILWAY MAPS

TOWN PLANS & DIAGRAMS

MAP DRAWING

ENGRAVING AND LITHOGRAPHING

MAP PRINTING

MAP MOUNTING

PARLIAMENTARY AND ESTATE PLANS

PLATES FOR SCIENTIFIC WORKS

ALL KINDS OF MAP WORK DRAWN ENGRAVED & PRINTED
COPIES OR CUTTINGS OF MAPS FOR SPECIAL PURPOSES
CAN BE PRINTED FROM A LARGE COLLECTION OF PLATES.

31 CHAMBERS STREET, EDINBURGH

Appendix I List of Directors

6th May 1919
(Statutory meeting at the incorporation of the company, John Bartholomew & Son Limited)

Dr J. G. Bartholomew (Chairman and managing director until his death in 1920)
A. G. Scott (a cousin of John George and formerly his sole partner in the business. He was responsible for the accounts. Died September 1938)
John Bartholomew ('Captain Ian', son of John George. He became chairman and managing director on his father's death in 1920. Died February 1962)
Thomas Barker (Printing manager, retired February 1933)
G. S. Robinson (Company secretary, retired February 1937)

16th March 1921

L. St C. Bartholomew (younger brother of John, resigned 1927)

1st February 1933

H. F. Rose (son-in-law of A. G. Scott, became in due course company secretary and accountant. A notable Bartholomew character, a stickler for protocol and routine. Residents of the Duncan Street neighbourhood set their watches by his passage, on foot, at seven every morning to his office—but first to the Post Office, to pick up the mail, which was not delivered early enough to suit his routine. When Mr Rose retired in March 1966 he devoted himself to his rock-garden, which was an Edinburgh curiosity because it was made up of discarded lithographic stones)

10th February 1939

A. Wishart, W.S. (a company lawyer, he died in 1943)
Mrs M. A. Bartholomew (wife of John. Resigned February 1953)

25th February 1944

Professor A. G. Ogilvie (Professor of geography at Edinburgh University. Resigned February 1953)

20th February 1953

John C. Bartholomew (eldest son of John)
Cartographic Director
W. J. Dickson (Production Manager, retired in March, 1966)

26th February 1954

Robert G. Bartholomew (third son of John)
Production Director

2nd March 1956

Peter H. Bartholomew (second son of John)
Chairman of the firm

24th February 1961

D. A. B. Cunningham Company Secretary and Financial Director

3rd February 1969

D. A. Ross Stewart Managing Director

11th February 1972

M. J. Chittleburgh Marketing Director

Two technical directors, were appointed in May 1967.
C. W. D. Kerr (Head Photographer) retired May 1970
and J. L. Colquhoun (Head Patcher) died May 1968

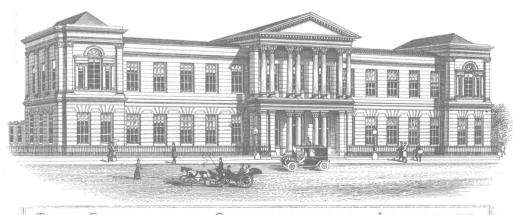

THE EDINBURGH GEOGRAPHICAL INSTITUTE.

Appendix II List of Long Serving Employees

Start	Finish		Department	Years Service
1878	1933	Thomas Barker	Production Manager	55
1883	1930	Charles Loch	Printer	47
1887	1936	James McVicar	Librarian	49
1887	1919	Thomas McDougall	Wareroom*	32
1887	1931	James Pollock	Engraver*	44
1887	1929	John Rennie	Patcher*	42
1889	1931	Adam Robertson	Printer*	42
1889	1920	James Stevens (Sen)	Mounting Manager	31
1895	1943	Francis Conacher	Office*	48
1896	1932	George Adamson	Printer	36
1897	1933	John Guthrie	Writer*	36
1897	1927	William Cockburn	Wareroom*	30
1900	1943	James Stevens (Jnr)	Transferrer	43
1900	1945	Robert Woodcock	Transferrer*	45
1901	1942	Georgina Russell	Mounter	41
1901	1937	Sarah Hutton	Layer-on	36
1902	1949	Jessie Thomson	Layer-on	47
1902	1945	Thomas Hay	Printer*	43
1902	1932	James Hewitt	Printer	30
1903	1940	Joan Muir	Mounter	37
1903	1945	Euphemia Cubie	Mounter	42
1904	1944	John Davidson	Transferrer	40
1905	1961	David Webster	Copperplate	55
1906	1944	Isabella Chisholm	Mounter	38
1906	1958	Alexander Knox	Engraver*	52
1906	1950	Edward Stanton	Paper	44
1907	1959	Maurice Meikle	Draughtsman	52
1908	1950	Martha Murdie	Mounter	42
1909	1962	John Davies	Engraver*	53
1909	1957	Charlotte Robertson	Wareroom	48
1910	1960	Elizabeth Cameron	Editorial	50
1910	1960	Allan Dick	Printer	50
1910	1947	Isabella Hogg	Mounter*	37
1910	1963	George Paterson	Printer*	52
1911	1953	Andrew Imrie	Writer*	42
1911	1956	Thomas Lyall	Draughtsman*	45
1911	1961	Robert Trotter	Transferrer*	50
1912	1961	Helen Imrie	Colourist	32
1912	1967	James Park	Office*	54
1912	1954	Walter Robinson	Mounting Manager	42
1912	1962	Alexander Williamson	Engraver/Draughtsman	50
1913	1963	Nan Tear	Colourist*	50
1914	1967	William Dickson	Production Manager	53
1915	1966	James Lewis	Draughtsman*	51
1915	1972	John Ramage	Draughtsman	48
1916	1958	Alexander Lawrie	Printer	42
1918	1956	David Russell	Printer*	38
1919	1957	John Shiels	Printer	38
1920	1964	John Bennett	Mounting Manager	44
1920	—	Helen Boyd	Office cleaner (part-time)	55
1921	1966	Frank Rose	Company Secretary	45
1921	1968	John Colquhoun	Patcher*	46
1924	1961	David Roberston	Stone Polisher	37
1924	1966	Francis Curle	Printer	42
1924	1973	Alexander Duff	Transferrer*	49
1924	1970	Ida Stewart	Colourist*	45
1929	—	Jean Dishington	Colourist	35
1929	1970	Isabel Mercer	Mounter*	40
1929	1960	Euphemia Runciman	Mounter	31
1930	1970	Clifford Kerr	Photo*	40

Start	Finish		Department	Years Service
1930	—	Thomas Cameron	Writer*	46
1931	—	David Webster	Engraver	45
1931	—	James Palmer	Printer*	30
1933	1968	Jessie Hairs	Mounter*	35
1933	1972	Willaim McConnell	Machine assistant	38
1935	—	Margaret Colthart	Colourist*	41
1936	—	Margaret Wilkinson	Colourist/Indexer	39
1936	—	James Mackay	Transferrer*	39
1937	1973	John Currie	Paper	35
1938	—	William Hall	Draughtsman*	38
1942	—	Margaret Livingston	Office	34
1945	—	Charles Roberston	Printer	30
1946	—	Peter Wilson	Engineer	30

*Departmental Head

Over 3000 years of loyal and devoted service

TELEGRAM ADDRESS,
"BARTHOLOMEW, EDINBURGH".

TELEPHONE
EDINBURGH 41911

Cartographers to the King

JOHN BARTHOLOMEW, F.R.G.S.
Managing Director

Appendix III List of Publications

I Atlas Publications

As the firm of Bartholomew did not set up its own printing presses until 1860, any atlas production prior to that date was in the form of engraved copper plates made up in page form and produced to the order of the publisher.

These included:

Adam & Charles Black, Edinburgh
Blackie & Son, London, Glasgow, etc.
William Blackwood & Sons, Edinburgh
Cambridge University Press, London
*Cassell & Company, London & New York
William Collins, Sons & Co, Glasgow
T & A Constable, Edinburgh
A Fullarton & Co., London & Edinburgh
*Hodder & Stoughton Ltd, London
W H Lizars Ltd., London

Macmillan & Co., London
Thomas Nelson & Sons, London & Edinburgh
George Newnes Ltd., London
*Oxford University Press, London
George Philip & Son, London & Liverpool
*The Reader's Digest Association, London, Sydney etc.
*The Times Publishing Co Ltd., London
John Thomson & Co., Edinburgh
John Walker & Co., London
T Ellwood Zell, Philadelphia

*Post 1892

It was not until Thomas Nelson died in 1892 that Bartholomews produced a catalogue listing their many atlases which were then being published by other publishers. Progressively after this time, atlases were published under the firm's own imprint. The major publications from both periods are listed below:

1832	Atlas of Scotland, engraved by W H Lizars and by George Bartholomew (Thomson)
1836	Lizar's General Atlas of the World, engraved by W H Lizars and by John Bartholomew Snr (Lizars)
1838	Blackwood's County Atlas of Scotland (Blackwood)
1853	Atlas of Australia with all the gold regions, engraved by S Hall, J Bartholomew and W Hughes (Black)
1856	Black's General Atlas of the World, and 1860, 1865, 1884 (Black)
1856	Black's Atlas of North America (Black)
1859	New Atlas of the World (Nelson)
1860	Royal Illustrated Atlas of Modern Geography, engraved by G H Swanston and by John Bartholomew Jnr (Fullarton)
1860	Imperial Atlas of Modern Geography (Blackie)
1862	Black's New Atlas of Scotland (Black)
	Philip's Imperial Library Atlas (Philip)
1871	Descriptive Hand Atlas of the World (Fullarton)
1873	Handy Atlas of the Counties of England (Philip)
1874	Handy General Atlas of the World, 1875 and 1885 (Philip)
1879	Philip's General Atlas of the World (Philip)
1879	Handy General Atlas of America (Philip)
1880	Baddeley's Guide to the English Lake District—*the first maps to use layer colouring* (Dulau & Co., London)
1880	International Atlas & Geography (Collins)
1881	Zell's Descriptive Hand Atlas of the World (Zell)
1882	Handy Atlas of the Counties of Scotland (Philip)
1886	Pocket Atlas of the World (John Walker); 2nd series of edition to 1901 and 3rd series of editions to 1942 (JB)
1886	Colonial Pocket Atlas (Walker) 3 editions to 1891
1887	Survey Gazetteer of the British Isles (A & C Black); 2nd edition 1904 (George Newnes and JB); 1913–3 editions to 1943 (JB)
1887	Handy Reference Atlas of the World, 9 editions to 1912 (Walker); 1923—7 editions to 1954 (JB)
1887	Pocket Atlas of England, 5 editions to 1897 (Walker)
1887	Pocket Atlas of Scotland, 3 editions to 1893 (Walker)
1887	Pocket Atlas of Ireland (Walker)
1888	Pocket Gazetteer of the World (Walker)
1889	Atlas of Commercial Geography (Cambridge University Press)

1889	Pocket Atlas & Guide to London, 16 editions to 1920 (Walker); 1922—10 editions to 1956 (JB)
1889	Pocket Atlas & Guide to Paris, 3 editions to 1898 (Walker)
1890	Library Reference Atlas of the World (Macmillan)
1890	Royal Atlas & Gazetteer of Australasia (Thos Nelson)
1890	Pocket Atlas of Canada, 2 editions to 1897 (Walker)
1890	Century Atlas & Gazeteer, 12 editions to 1911 (Walker)
1891	Graphic Atlas (Nelson); 1893, 1910 (Walker); 1932—9 editions to 1956 (JB)
1891	Popular Hand Atlas of the World (Nelson)
1891	English Imperial Atlas of the World (Nelson)
1892	Miniature Atlas & Gazeteer (Nelson); 1894 (Walker)
1892	Handy Atlas of England & Wales (Black)
1893	New Hand Atlas of India (Arch Constable)
1893	Atlas Guide to Europe (Philip)
1895	Survey Atlas of Scotland, 2nd edition 1912
1897	Melrose and Abbotsford Pocket Guide, 4 editions to 1924
1898	Citizen's Atlas (Newnes) and 1901; 1912—8 editions to 1952 (JB)
1899	Atlas of Meteorology
1899	Royal Atlas of England & Wales (Newnes)
1903	Pocket Atlas of the British Isles (Newnes) and 1906; 1918—13 editions to 1958 (JB)
1904	Survey Atlas of England & Wales, 2nd edition 1912
1904	Handy Atlas of the British Empire (Newnes)
1906	Ideal Atlas of the World, 3 editions to 1912 (Walker)
1906	Climatological Atlas of India
1907	Handy Reference Atlas of London (Walker); 1913 to 1917; 1921—10 editions to 1968 (JB)
1907	Atlas of the World's Commerce (Newnes)
1908	Imperial Gazetteer Atlas of India, and 1931 (Oxford University Press)
1909	Cassell's Atlas of the World (Cassell)
1911	Atlas of Zoogeography
1914	International Reference Atlas (Newnes)
1915	Atlas of the Historical Geography of the Holy Land (Hodder & Stoughton)
1922	Pocket Atlas and Guide to Glasgow (John Smith, Glasgow)
1922	Times Survey Atlas of the World (Times)
1923	Birmingham Pocket Atlas, 9 editions to 1923
1924	Universal Hand Atlas (Nelson)
1927	Manchester Pocket Atlas
1928	Liverpool & Birkenhead Pocket Atlas, and 1949
1934	Newnes Modern World Atlas (Newnes)
1935	The Times Handy Atlas (Times)
1943	Compact Atlas of the World, 4 editions to 1957
1943	Road Atlas of Great Britain, 22 editions to 1970
1948	Regional Atlas of the World
1950	Edinburgh Atlas Guide, 6 editions to 1974
1953	Columbus Atlas of the World
1954	Edinburgh World Atlas, 10 editions to 1975
1955–60	The Times Atlas of the World (Mid-Century edition), in 5 volumes (Times)
1958	Roadmaster Atlas of Great Britain, 5 editions to 1971
1961	Reader's Digest Great World Atlas, British edition and subsequent special language editions for Australia, Brazil, Canada, Denmark, Finland, France, Germany, Italy, Japan, Mexico, The Netherlands, Norway, Spain, Sweden and USA (Reader's Digest)
1967	The Times Atlas of the World (Comprehensive Edition); 5 editions to 1975 (Times); also German editions 1972, 1974 and 1976
1969	The Times Moon Atlas (Times)
1970	Road Atlas Britain, 7 editions to 1976
1970	Road Atlas Europe, 4 editions to 1974
1972	The Times Concise Atlas of the World; 5 editions to 1975; also Dutch editions 1973 and 1975; and German edition 1976 (Times)
1973	Town Plan Atlas
1973	Motorway Atlas, 2 editions to 1975
1974	The Times Atlas of China (Times)
1974	Atlas of Europe (published jointly with Frederick Warne)

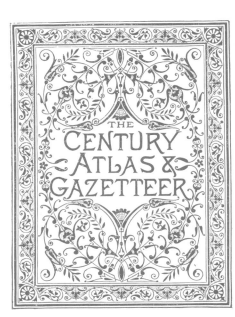

Appendix III

II Map Publications

As with atlas publications, maps were initially produced for other publishers and A & C Black, who were neighbours in North Bridge, Edinburgh, were the main outlet for Bartholomew productions up to 1884, when John Walker & Co of London and W H Smith (particularly through their railway bookstalls) jointly took over the publication and distribution. Gradually during the 1890's the firm published an increasing number of new maps under its own name. The following list is a selection of the more important titles:

1826	Lothian's Plan of the Town of Leith. Engraved by George Bartholomew
1826	Directory Plan of Edinburgh. Engraved by John Bartholomew Snr
1834–45	Blackwood's County Maps for the Second Statistical Account of Scotland
1846	Plan of Edinburgh engraved on steel by John Bartholomew Snr. for W. & H. Lizars
1862	Black's Large Tourist Map of Scotland in 12 sheets, 4 miles to the inch
1865	Directory Plan of Glasgow, 6 inches to the mile
1866	Black's New Large Map of England & Wales
1868	Directory Plan of Edinburgh, 6 inches to the mile
1868	London & Environs. 4 miles to the inch. Political (1911 Physical)
1871	Directory Plan of Greenock, 6 inches to the mile
1871	London Plan, $3\frac{1}{4}$ inches to the mile (1907 enlarged area in 4 sheets)
1871	Aldershot & Environs, 4 miles to the inch (1881 2 miles to the inch)
1873	General Railway Map of the British Isles
1874	Directory Plan of Dundee, 6 inches to the mile
1875–86	Reduced Ordnance Survey Maps of Scotland in 30 'District' sheets— 2 miles to the inch
1876	Tourist Map of Scotland, 10 miles to the inch. Political (1909 Physical)
1877	Yorkshire, 4 miles to the inch
1877	London Environs, 1 inch to the mile. Physical
1881	Commercial and Library Chart of the World (Philip)
1883	Directory Plan of Paisley, 6 inches to the mile
1888–96	Chambers' Encyclopaedia Maps (Lippincott of Philadelphia)
1889	Pocket Plan of Edinburgh, $3\frac{1}{2}$ inches to the mile
1890	Pocket Plan of Glasgow, 5 inches to the mile
1890	Political Map of Africa, 1:12 mil. (1949—1:10 mil. Physical)
1890	Reduced Ordnance Survey Maps of Scotland—new series in 29 sheets 2 miles to the inch
1890	Pentland Hills Map, $1\frac{1}{2}$ inches to the mile
1891	Reduced Survey Map of India, 1:$4\frac{1}{2}$ mil. (Thacker & Co.)
1891	Touring Map of Central Europe 1:2 mil. Political (1914—Physical)
1891	Map of British South Africa, 1:5.6 mil.
1891	Large Plan of Edinburgh in 12 sheets. 15 inches to the mile. Sheet 8 (1885)
1891	Reduced Ordnance Map of the British Isles, 10 miles to the inch (Philip)
1892	Geological Map of Scotland. 10 miles to the inch
1892	Statesman Yearbook Maps (Macmillan)
1893	Naturalist's Map of Scotland, 10 miles to the inch
1893	Lake District, 3 miles to the inch. Physical (1913 1 inch to the mile made up from 1881 Windermere and 1883 Keswick)
1894	Distillery Map of Scotland (Chas Mackinlay)
1894	Map of South America, 1:12 mil. (1900—1:10 mil)
1895	Australia—Commercial Map, 1:6 mil.
1896	World Route Chart
1896–1904	Quarter-inch Map of Ireland in 7 sheets (1949, rearranged in 5 sheets)
1897	Quarter-inch Map of England & Wales in 12 sheets
1897–1903	Half-inch Map of England and Wales in 37 sheets
1898	Geological Map of England & Wales. 10 miles to the inch
1898	South Africa, 1:$2\frac{1}{2}$ mil. Physical
1900	Quarter-inch Map of Palestine Physical
1901–07	Maps for Murray's Bathymetrical Survey of Scottish Freshwater Lochs
1905	Europe and the Mediterranean, 1:5 mil. Political
1906	Geological Map of Ireland. 10 miles to the inch
1907	British Isles. Contoured Motoring Map, 1:1 mil.
1907	Botanical Survey of Scotland

1907	Channel Islands. Physical
1910	France, 1:1 mil. Physical
1910–11	Quarter-inch Map of Scotland in 7 sheets
1912	United States, 1:5 mil. Physical
1915	Egypt, 1:1 mil. Hill-shading
1915	Italy & Balkans, 1:2 mil. Physical
1916	Switzerland and Italian Lakes. 8 miles to the inch. Physical
1917	New Zealand, 1:2 mil. Physical
1917	India, 1:4 mil. Physical
1922	Australia, South Eastern, 1:2½ mil. Physical
1922	Spain and Portugal, 25 miles to the inch Physical (1969, 1:1¼ mil, hill shading)
1922	Middle East 1:4 mil. Physical
1922	North America, 1:10 mil. Political (1957 Physical)
1922	Malaya and Indo-China, 1:4 mil. Physical
1923	Pocket Plan of Glasgow, 2½ inches to the mile
1923	Japan, 1:3 mil. Physical (1963 1:2½ mil)
1925	England and Wales Touring, 12 miles to the inch. Physical
1926	Germany, Holland and Belgium, 1:1 mil. Physical
1927	Scotland Touring. 12 miles to the inch. Physical
1928	Western Europe, 1:3 mil. Physical
1929	London & Home Counties AA Duplex Throughway Map. ('To & Through' series 1971) (1932 Birmingham; 1956 Manchester, Liverpool, Leeds & Sheffield; 1973 Edinburgh & Glasgow, 1976 Bristol, Cardiff, Swansea, Southampton)
1929–33	Quarter-inch AA Map of Great Britain in 23 sheets
1930	Ireland Touring, 12 miles to the inch. Physical
1933	Pictorial Fisherman's Maps of Tay, Tweed, Dee and Spey
1933	Eastern Europe, 1:3 mil. Physical
1937	The Royal River, an illustrated map of the Thames
1937	Half-inch Scotland. New lay-out in 25 sheets, renumbered with a view to combining with England & Wales to form one series
1938	Children's Historical Map of London (1939 England; 1946 Scotland; 1947 United Nations; 1962 Ireland; 1966 Wales; 1969 London)
1940	Scandinavia, 1:3 mil. Physical
1941	Far East and Western Pacific, 1:10 mil. Physical
1942	Burma, Malaya & Indo-China, 1:4 mil. Physical
1942	China & Japan, 1:6 mil. Physical
1942	Iceland, 1:750 000. Physical
1942	Russia in Europe, 1:4½ mil. Physical
1942	Half-inch Great Britain Series in 62 sheets, numbering from South to North
1955	RAC Motoring Map of Great Britain in 8 sheets 6 miles to the inch (1969 renamed Tourmaster Series)
1960	Scotland of Old (Clan Map)
1963	London, Westminster to the City. 9 inches to the mile (renamed London Central Pocket Map)
1963	Central Europe, 1:1¼ mil. Hill-shading
1963	Eurasia, 1:15 mil. Physical
1964	Asia, South-East, 1:5.8 mil
1967	Early Map Reproductions taken from Blaeu's *Atlas Maior*
1968	Israel, 1:350 000. Physical
1970	Grand Touring (GT) Series in 10 sheets, 4 miles to the inch
1971	The Mapping of Scotland—facsimile reproductions of early maps to the 19th century, prepared for the IVth International Conference on the History of Cartography, Edinburgh 1971
1972	The Times World Wall Map
1972	Edinburgh City Plan, 1:15 000
1973	The World, 1:30 mil. Political
1973	Tourist Route Series of Great Britain in 3 sheets, 9 miles to the inch
1974	Motorway Map of the British Isles, 1:1¼ mil.
1974	West Indies & the Caribbean, 1:3¼ mil.
1974	Counties, Regions & Districts of the British Isles, 1:1¼ mil.
1975	National Map Series in 62 sheets, 1:100 000 (based on the half-inch series)
1976	Everyone's London Plan, 1:15 000

TOURIST'S & SPORTSMAN'S SERIES

BARTHOLOMEW'S REDUCED ORDNANCE SURVEY MAPS OF SCOTLAND

Appendix III

III Educational Atlases

A large proportion of Bartholomew production over the last hundred years has been taken up with providing school atlases for the educational market, which market really started to blossom towards the end of the 19th century. In this period, most of this production was supplied to four educational publishers. Between them, they purchased over 12 million atlases, the largest being Oxford University Press with over 4 million atlases (their Indian School Atlas over 2 million copies in 22 editions). Meiklejohn & Son with 3 million atlases (of which over 2 million copies are represented by the Comparative Atlas published in 50 editions. J M Dent & Sons, also with 3 million atlases (of which their Canadian School Atlas accounted for 2½ million copies), and lastly, Thomas Nelson & Son with 1½ million atlases spread over a great number of publications. In addition to atlases, wall maps for schools were produced in their hundreds of thousands. Unfortunately, detailed records prior to 1869 have not been retained, but below is given a list of school atlases in chronological order of their first edition.

1869	School Atlas	A & C Black
	One Shilling Atlas	Chambers
	New Atlas	Fullarton
1870	Sixpenny Atlas	Chambers
	Victoria Atlas	Collins
	Outline Atlas	Heywood
	Blank Atlas	Heywood
1871	Beginners Atlas	Black
1872	Atlas Historique de Belgique (2 editions to 1889)	Manceau
1873	Handy General Atlas	Philip
	Colonial Atlas	Philip
1875	Junior Atlas	Jarrold
1888	Nouvel Atlas de Belgique	Lebègue
1890	Physical & Political School Atlas	Macmillan
1891	School Hand Atlas 'Globe' (6 editions to 1899)	Nelson
1891	Royal Shilling Atlas (11 editions to 1911)	Nelson
1892	Elementary School Atlas	Macmillan
	One Shilling Atlas (16 editions to 1914)	Nelson
	One Shilling School Atlas—India (23 editions to 1916)	Nelson
	One Shilling School Atlas—Canadian	Nelson
	Atlas de Géographie Moderne de Belgique (2 editions to 1901)	Lebègue
1893	Charterhouse Atlas (8 editions to 1909)	Relfe Brothers
1894	Aldersgate Atlas (2 editions to 1898)	Relfe Brothers
	Satchel School Atlas (2 editions to 1897)	Walker
1897	One Shilling School Atlas—S Africa (15 editions to 1916)	Nelson
	Indian School Atlas (4 editions to 1911)	Macmillan
1898	Comparative Atlas (50 editions to 1971)	Meiklejohn
1900	Indian Primary School Atlas	Macmillan
1901	International Students' Atlas	Newnes
	Chinese School Atlas (2 editions to 1904)	Macmillan
1903	Advanced South African Atlas	Nelson
1904	Royal Shilling Atlas—Canadian (7 editions to 1915)	Nelson
1905	Historical Atlas of the British Empire	Methuen
1910	School Economic Atlas (14 editions to 1950)	Oxford University Press
	Literary & Historical Atlas of Europe (3 editions to 1923)	Dent
1911	Literary & Historical Atlas of America (2 editions to 1930)	Dent
1912	Literary & Historical Atlas of Asia	Dent
1913	Literary & Historical Atlas of Africa & Australia	Dent
	Atlas of Ancient & Classical Geography (6 editions to 1960)	Dent
	Shilling School Atlas (2 editions to 1915)	Oxford University Press
1915	Indian School Atlas (22 editions to 1976)	Oxford University Press

	Australasian School Atlas (17 editions to 1966)	Oxford University Press
	Historical Atlas of Modern Europe (2 editions to 1923)	Oxford University Press
	Oxford Advanced Atlas (12 editions to 1947)	Oxford University Press
1920	Royal Atlas for Indian Schools (6 editions to 1931)	Nelson
	Royal Atlas for Canadian Schools (6 editions to 1924)	Nelson
1921	Australian Primary Atlas	Oxford University Press
1923	Canadian School Atlas (46 editions to 1975)	Dent
	General School Atlas (5 editions to 1938)	Harrap
	Canadian Junior School Atlas	Dent
1925	Historical Atlas of Canada	Nelson
1928	Preparatory School Atlas	Oxford University Press
1929	Nelson's School Atlas	Nelson
	Economic Atlas of USA	Oxford University Press
1933	New World Atlas (2 editions to 1938)	Harrap
1934	Indian 'Tamil' School Atlas (7 editions to 1955)	Oxford University Press
	Indian 'Telugu' School Atlas (4 editions to 1955)	Oxford University Press
	Canadian School Atlas (11 editions to 1955)	Nelson
1937	Modern School Atlas	Harrap
1938	Indian 'Bengali' School Atlas (2 editions to 1951)	Oxford University Press
	Indian 'Marathi' School Atlas (3 editions to 1953)	Oxford University Press
	Indian 'Urdu' School Atlas	Oxford University Press
1940	Irish Students Atlas	Educational Company of Ireland
	Intermediate School Atlas	Meiklejohn
1946	Indian 'Hindi' School Atlas (4 editions to 1954)	Oxford University Press
1949	Advanced Atlas of Modern Geography (4 editions to 1957)	Meiklejohn
1952	Canadian Social Studies Atlas (7 editions to 1969)	Dent
1959	Advanced Atlas of Modern Geography (6 editions to 1973)	Oliver & Boyd
1961	Aldine World Atlas (5 editions to 1974)	Dent
1972	Exploration Universe ("Our World")	Jointly with Holmes McDougall
1975	Problems of Our Planet	Jointly with Holmes McDougall

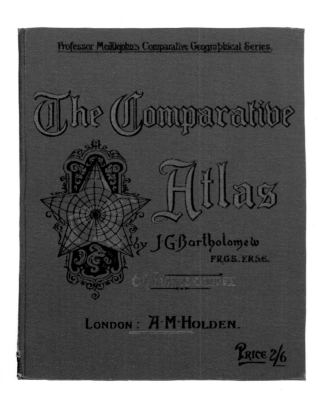

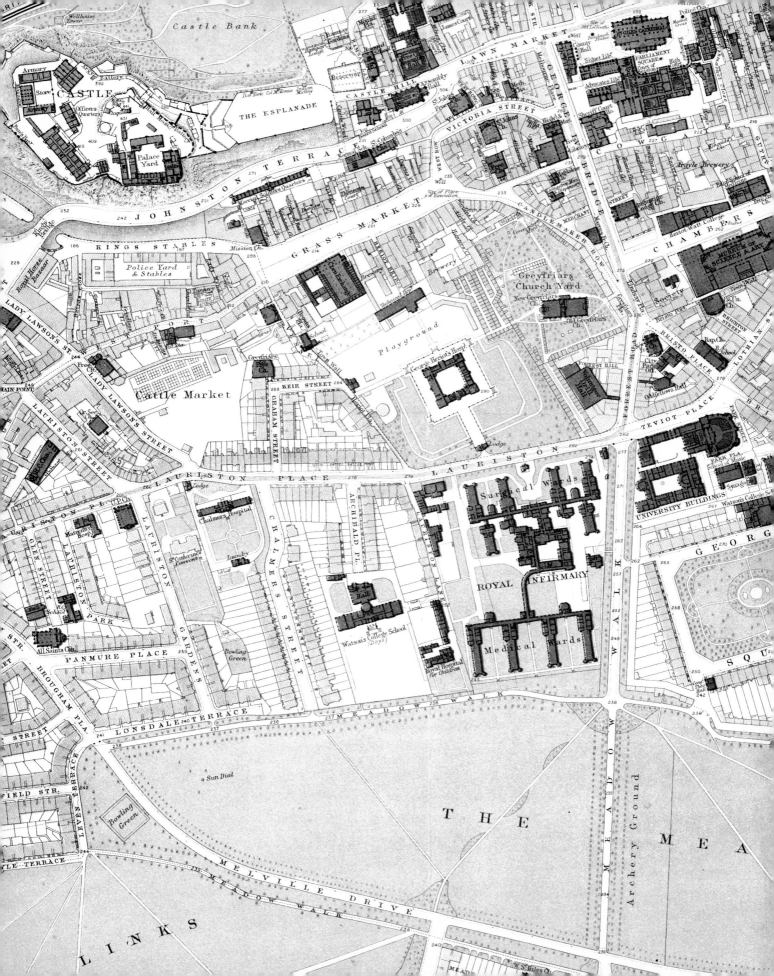